跨文化学习系列读本·商务实战篇

老　青　王晓明　主编

世界知识出版社

图书在版编目(CIP)数据

跨文化学习系列读本．商务实战篇／老青，王晓明主编．
—北京：世界知识出版社，2015.5

ISBN 978-7-5012-4915-2

Ⅰ．①跨…　Ⅱ．①老…②王…　Ⅲ．①风俗习惯—世界
Ⅳ．①K891

中国版本图书馆 CIP 数据核字（2015）第 097355 号

世界知识出版社
（北京市东城区干面胡同 51 号 100010）

责任编辑　柏　英

责任出版　王勇刚

责任校对　马莉娜

北京京华虎彩印刷有限公司

网址：www.wap1934.com

电话：010-65265923（发行）　010-85119023（邮购）

经销：新华书店

开本：680×980 毫米　1/16

印张：18　　字数 213 千

2015 年 5 月第一版　2015 年 5 月第一次印刷

标准书号　ISBN 978-7-5012-4915-2

定价：36.00 元

编委会

主　编：老　青　王晓明

副主编：刘晓晶　谢金艳　程云艳

编　者：王月会　康宁琨　刘素琴

王金环　刘钊宏　丁潇君

杨志强　梁穗明　徐小丽

前 言

中国经济实力不断增强，能源行业随中国经济这艘大船乘风破浪，进一步驶向远洋、跨越全球。能源行业国际化进程发展不仅体现在企业战略的扩张之中，更体现在其担负国家能源战略与能源安全的使命之中。这意味着国际竞争与博弈更加激烈，企业可以选择在世界上任何地方做生意，价格和质量是一种考量，双方的合作态度与跨文化交流的能力也起决定作用。因此，了解和掌握在英语语言环境下与客户国家开展商务交流的相关知识与业务合作的有效策略是非常必要的。

作为“跨文化学习系列读本”之一的《商务实战篇》，顺应“一带一路”战略，根据中国能源行业领域合作开展的境外工作需要，紧密围绕岗位核心能力，按照主题演讲、商务谈判、合同读译、工作报告、会议速记、论坛口译等有序编排，各章内构建学以致用模式，即“imput”引领为先，“output”指导为终，以习读为出发点，以应用为落脚点；书后配以网站信息翻译纠错解析和OPEC组织相关信息资料等附录内容，旨在促进能源行业领域国际化战略人才培养与潜力拓展、提高中国企业国际合作交往的实效。

本书是中国职业技术教育学会教学工作委员会2014—2015年职业教育英语类教学改革实践研究课题重点项目（主持人：老青）的成果之一，受到了北京市高端技术技能人才培养模式改革专项的资助。参与本书编著的主要人员来自中国社会科学院研究生院、北京青年政治学院、北京第二外国语学院、北京经济管理职业学院、河北廊坊燕京职业技术学院等。

在本书编写中我们得到了中国海洋石油服务股份有限公司、北京燕山石化有限公司培训中心、广东宝达游艇制造有限公司、广州海关，以及北京市教育委员会、北京工业大学、北京语言大学、中华女子学院的大力支持与帮助，在此表示衷心的感谢！特别感谢世界知识出版社编审柏英长期的支持、指导与帮助！由于编者水平有限，本书中难免有不当和疏漏之处，希望专家、同行及广大读者批评指正。

老青　王晓明

2015年3月31日

目 录

第一章　主题演讲

主题演讲是报告人面向听众，针对某一主题做出介绍、分析、评价或总结，并发表指导意见的讲话。主题演讲具有交流思想、通报情况、报告工作、教育群众、鼓动群众等作用。演讲人通过富有说服力的语言和演讲技巧，可以引起听众的关注和追捧，从而一举成名或者助力实现个人目的。比如，美国现任总统巴拉克·奥巴马在 2004 年美国民主党全国代表大会发表主题演讲“无畏的希望”（The Audacity of Hope）引起轰动，一跃而成闻名全美的政界人物，为其在党内的地位奠定了坚实的基础，从而顺利进入总统选举的角斗场，最终成为美国历史上第一位黑人总统。主题演讲还经常用于高等院校的开学或毕业典礼，一般由该校的杰出校友或者政要明星对全体学生进行演讲，以鼓舞和激励学生发奋图强、实现自我价值。比如，美国最著名的脱口秀女王奥普拉·温弗瑞 2013 年应邀出席哈佛大学毕业典礼并发表主题演讲，她用诚挚热情又不失诙谐幽默的演讲风格与哈佛学子们分享自己的人生阅历与成功经验，鼓励毕业生们在面临困境时要保持头脑清醒，时刻牢记作为公民的责任与仁爱之心。

在商业情境中，主题演讲通常用于正式的商务活动（business events）、国际会议（international conferences or congresses）和行业研讨（seminars），相比一般的会议报告具有更为重大的作用。主题演讲为会议议程确立主题和框架，归纳核心议题，即为整个会议定下基调（set the underlying tone）。比如，第 21 届世界石油大会于 2014 年 6 月在莫斯科落下帷幕，这场被称为“石油圈的奥林匹克”的盛会以“负责任地提供能源、强力支持发展中的世界”为主题，契合了当时各方关切，成为热议话题。世界石油巨头英国石油集团（BP）的首席技术官大卫·艾顿（David Eyton）在大会上做了题为“技术优势——科学和技术将如何改变我们发现、产生和使用能源的方式”（*The technical edge — how science and technology will transform the way we find, produce and use energy*）的主题演讲。在演讲中，他回顾了世界能源需求、新技术的必要性、新时期的挑战，结合实例阐明了BP在应用新技术加速能源供应、进行生态系统创新的举措，并提出世界范围内合作共赢的战略设想。演讲逻辑缜密、层次清晰、内容翔实，加上大卫·艾顿自信而富有感染力的表达，为BP公司增色不少。

不同的场合之下主题演讲的长度有所不同，一般分为长篇演讲和短篇演讲。短篇演讲3—5分钟，300—500词左右，主要用于一般公共场合，如大学开学或毕业典礼、庆祝活动等的开场。内容简洁明了，语言表达上倾向于轻松、幽默、有感染力，重在引起听众的共鸣。长篇主题演讲通常用在专业性较强的正式场合，如国际会议和研讨会等，报告15—30分钟，就某一专题进行较为深入的剖析和评述，阐述如前段做了什么、结果如何，或分析当前的形势、明确今后的任务，或表明对某事某问题的观点、看法，申述自己的主张，或说明会议的重要意义等，需要旗帜鲜明地表明看法，进行阐述，做出评价和总结。语言表达上更为正式、客观，重在说服听众接受自己的观点。

一、主题演讲的标题部分

（一）直接式主题演讲标题

直接式主题演讲标题直接表明某人在某演讲中的宗旨，也可以把演讲人的姓名放在标题之下，标题只标明在某会议上的演讲。例如：

David Eyton Keynote Speech to the Chinese Academy of Engineering（大卫·伊顿在中国工程院的主题演讲）

Energy Outlook 2030 Opening Remark（2030年能源展望开场报告）

Report by Geoff Morrell at the Society of Environmental Journalists Conference（杰奥夫·摩瑞尔在环境协会记者会上的演讲）

（二）文章主题式主题演讲标题

文章主题式演讲标题是用途最为广泛的一种标题方式，即根据演讲的主题，拟定一个题目。题目可以是一个关键词构成的名词短语、介词短语、动名词短语，也可以是一个陈述句、疑问句或设问句。

名词短语做标题，例如：

Energy Trends and Transitions in Asia（亚洲能源趋势和转型）

Reflections for the Next Generation of Energy professionals（下一代能源专家的思考）

Future Trends in Global Oil and Gas Exploration（全球油气开采的未来趋势）

A Road Map for America's Energy Future（美国能源前景路线图）

介词短语做标题，例如：

From Energy Crisis to Energy Security（从能源危机到能源安全）

Towards the Energy Future（迈向能源的未来）

动名词短语做标题，例如：

Delivering Energy in the 21st Century（21世纪的能源传输）

Creating Opportunity and Solving Challenges through Technology, Teamwork and Know-How（依靠技术、团队和专业知识创造机会，应对挑战）

Managing Risk and Building Value in the Next Decade（未来十年的风险管理和价值创造）

Making Intelligent Energy Happen（实现智能能源）

陈述句、疑问句或设问句做标题，例如：

A Healthy America Needs a Healthy Energy Industry（健康的美国需要健康的能源业）

How Science and Technology Will Transform the Way We Find, Produce and Use Energy（科技

如何改变能源发掘、生产和利用?)

How to Expand Energy Supply in the 21st Century?(21世纪如何扩大能源供给?)

Will Unconventional Oil and Gas Impact Deepwater Developments?(非常规油气资源会影响深海开发吗?)

(三) 主副标题式主题演讲标题

主副标题式主题演讲标题以文章式标题为正题，揭示演讲的主旨，副标题标明演讲者姓名和演讲的场合。或者由两个短语构成，分别为主题词和附加补充信息，两者用冒号或者破折号隔开。

China's Energy Future－Bob Dudley's Speech to Tsinghua University(中国能源前景：鲍勃·杜德利在清华大学的演讲)

Challenging Opportunities: The US, Russia and the World's Energy Journey(挑战机遇并存：美国、俄罗斯和世界能源之路)

Europe Energy Crisis: Pathways to a Resolution(欧洲能源危机：解决途径)

The Changing Global Energy Landscape－Prospects for Arctic Oil and Gas(全球能源版图变迁——北极油气资源前景)

The Energy Roadmap－Setting the Direction

for 21st Century Energy（能源路线图——21世纪能源方向导引）

二、主题演讲的正文部分

主题演讲的正文由称呼语、开场白、主体、结尾三部分组成。

（一）称呼语

演讲开始时对听众的称呼语，表达问候和感谢。最常用的是“Ladies and gentlemen”，也可根据不同情况，选用“Fellow students”“Distinguished guests”“Mr. Chairman”“Honorable Judges”等。例如：

Good afternoon ladies and gentlemen and thank you for inviting me to join this seminar today.

Thank you for the invitation to speak at your conference celebrating the centenary of Oil Technology at Imperial College. It is an honour and great pleasure to be here.

称呼语后可以用几句诚恳的语句与听众建立个人间的关系，获得听众的好感和信任。例如：

It is always marvelous to come back to Stanford and it is a pleasure and a privilege to be here to speak to you today on a subject which I believe, is of the utmost importance. I can't think of anywhere better than Stanford to discuss in a calm and rational way a subject which raises great emotion and which requires both analysis and action.

这是英国石油公司一位高层在斯坦福大学所做的关于全球气候变化的主题演讲。开场时演讲人就明确提出斯坦福大学是研究本课题的最好的地方，以此博得听众的认同感，吸引听众进入演讲正题。

（二）开场白

开场白是演讲稿中很重要的部分。好的开场白能够紧紧地抓住听众的注意力，为整场主题演讲的成功打下基础。常用的开场白有点明主题、交代背景、提出问题等。不论哪种开场白，目的都是使听众立即了解主题、引入正文、引起思考等。常用的开场白有如下几种：

1. 开门见山，提示主题。

这种开头是一开讲，就进入正题，直接提示演讲的中心。运用这种方法，必须先明晰地把握演讲的中心，把要向听众提示的论点摆出来，使听众一听就知道讲的中心是什么，注意力马上集中起来。例如：

I'll start with a broad overview of the outlook for oil and gas, then look at how technology can contribute towards meeting the major challenges facing the industry, and finally touch on the importance of regional differences.

演讲人分别用“start with”“then”“finally”提示他要讨论的三个议题，简洁明了，层次清晰，让听众一目了然。例如：

I will try to keep you awake by first debunking a few myths about energy, then by making a few predictions — and finally by explaining why the company that invests more than any other in American energy wants to carry on doing just that for many years to come. (No prizes for guessing which company that is.)

演讲人用“first”“then”和“finally”连接三个由“by+doing”的并列结构提示主题，同时还玩了一把小幽默，如：

Keep you awake. (希望听众不要听睡着了。)

No prizes for guessing which company that is. (猜中公司名称没有奖励。)

这可以让听众在开怀一笑中明确了演讲的主题。

2. 现身说法，衔接主题。

这种开头通常是用自己的经历引出主题，现身说法可以迅速缩短与听众的距离，引起听众共鸣，同时吸引听众了解下文。例如：

It is a great honour, as a representative of BP—and as a native of Delhi. For me, this is a chance to come home and to reflect on the extraordinary journey of growth that India has undertaken. When I was growing up here in the 1970s, the population of

Delhi was about 4 million with about 100,000 cars on the roads. Today, Delhi's population is over 17 million, with over one-and-a-half million cars on the roads. Such rapid growth creates challenges, but also solutions. Some are perhaps straight forward, such as the conversion of vehicles to compressed natural gas which has reduced levels of sulphur dioxide.

演讲人首先摆明自己是家乡人的身份，和听众拉近距离，之后以自己亲身经历描述家乡的变迁，最后自然地过渡到演讲的主题：经济快速发展产生的能源挑战和应对措施。

3. 提出问题，引起关注。

这种方法是根据听众的特点和演讲的内容，提出一些激发听众思考的问题，以引起听众的注意。例如：

In seeking to set out a basis for addressing these issues, I will focus on three questions:

What is the energy challenge?

What should be the policy response?

And what should be the business response?

演讲人围绕主题接连提出三个问题：何谓能源挑战？决策领域如何应对？行业领域如何应对？一连串的问题势必会激起听众的好奇和求知欲，吸引听众跟随报告追寻答案。例如：

First then, what is the dilemma? It is sometimes referred to as a 'tri-lemma' because it comprises three questions.

Is there enough energy to meet global demand?

Does each country know where its supplies will come from?

And finally, can supplies be delivered without unacceptable impact on the planet's ecosystem?

演讲人巧妙地运用构词的异化，将主题词“di-lemma”转换成适合情境的“tri-lemma”，并由此提出“tri-questions”。

（三）主体

这是主题演讲的重点内容，即对开场提出的主题或问题进行情况说明、原因分析，并提出解决方案或途径。对提出的论题，不可主观地妄下结论，而要进行客观的论证。这是主题演讲中最需要下功夫的部分，关键是得把道理讲清楚。主题演讲以演讲形式进行论证，即语言输入速度较快，为了让听众能够集中精力、跟上节奏、听得明白，论证部分尽量用 first, second, third 的列举式来序化观点，语言的运用上除了必须要使用的专业术语之外，以简单词汇和短小句型为主。例如：

I see four areas in which policy-makers might take action to stimulate the technology and partnerships required.

The first is to create the right "above ground" conditions. By this I mean creating the right policy frameworks to incentivize competition and investment. This can embrace everything from regulatory frameworks to public－private partnerships. This is one of the greatest lessons from the US shale revolution.

The second area for action is to enable the right price signals to prevail. The recent gas price notification is a welcome step. But the further the country can move towards free market pricing, the more it can increase domestic supply, reduce imports and improve the trade imbalance.

The third area for action is to create a means to an end — to focus on the journey as well as the destination. Renewables may well be a large part of the answer in the long term — and they can meet specific needs today—I am mindful of TERI's great work with solar power in rural areas. But in the short to medium term, the best way to bring emissions down at scale is to bring up the proportion of gas in the energy mix and bring down energy intensity. In other words, the amount of energy needed to generate one unit of GDP.

The fourth area is to support the market in stimulating the creation of supply chains that provide the capability and expertise to deliver energy. In many countries, the US and UK included, investment in domestic energy has led to service industries being created. In others, such as Trinidad and Azerbaijan, local fabrication industries have emerged.

如上所示，演讲人首先用最直接的方式点明要阐述的四个内容（I see four areas in which policy-makers might take action to），之后分别用“the first” “the second” “the third”和“the fourth”依次论述观点，同时，演讲人还对一些比较难以理解的概念进行释义，以加深听众的印象。如在说到第一个观点（create the right “above ground”conditions）时，听众很可能对“above ground”的提法感到疑惑，报告人随即附加解释“By this I mean creating the right policy frameworks to incentivisze competition and investment”，听众便会明白，“above ground”是相对石油行业而言的，因为石油开采都是在地下进行，即“beneath ground”，演讲人提出地上即是上层政策框架的创建，以刺激石油行业的竞争和投资。

三、主题演讲的结尾部分

主题演讲的结尾结论要简明扼要，以给听众留下深刻印象。通常结尾包括总结重申演讲的观点，展望前景或发出号召，并感谢听众的关注。例如：

> Let me conclude by widening the lens once again, this time not to look at the energy industry but at society as whole.
>
> As I conclude, let me add that BP has a long history in India, spanning over 100 years with our castrol lubricants brand. We have a number of

people in the group — around 5,000 — working in India supporting our global, technology and financial operations. And more recently we have been very pleased to have the opportunity to participate more directly in India's energy future.

To notch down my feelings for a moment, and to conclude, I am confident that the energy sector can meet the challenge of fueling the future generations of the globe.

Winston Churchill said: "A pessimist sees the difficulty in every opportunity; an optimist sees the opportunity in every difficulty." And when it comes to our industry's capacity to overcome difficulties and supply the energy that the world needs for its growth and development, whether from the Arctic or elsewhere, I am very much an optimist.

下面，以现任英国石油集团（BP）和沃尔沃集团（Volvo）董事长在哈佛大学肯尼迪政府学院政治研究所的肯尼迪论坛上发表的完整报告，题目《应对能源挑战》为范例予以整体解析。

Facing the Energy Challenge

Speaker: Carl-Henric Svanberg

Speech date: 13 November 2012

Venue: John F. Kennedy Forum at the Institute of Politics at Harvard's Kennedy School of Government

It is always good to be here in Harvard and to be at the Kennedy School. In few other places will you find so many brilliant people with such a passion for problem-solving. And I speak as a member of the Dean's Council and the parent of a recent student. So I am here to listen as well as to talk.

开场白中，报告人对学院不吝赞美，高度评价肯尼迪学院对研究问题解决问题的热情。同时表明身份，即是院长委员会的一员，又是学院一位新生的家长，和肯尼迪学院可谓关系密切，以此拉近和听众的距离，增加亲切感和认同感。

Today's topic is "Facing the energy challenge". I am going to address this from the perspective of the two companies that I chair：BP，the energy supplier；and Volvo Group，the manufacturer of commercial trucks，buses and construction equipment. These companies represent the whole energy chain from what we call "wells to wheels".

开门见山，点明主题：应对能源挑战。现身说法，同时作为能源业翘楚英国石油集团和汽车业巨头沃尔沃集团的董事长，将以自身的思考来剖析问题。其中"well to wheels"的说法极为巧妙，头尾押韵、朗朗上口，并且揭示了能源链的起始和末端，而报告人在这两个领域里均有丰富的知识储备和管理经验，暗示听众报告人的论述将会是客观深入、令人信服的。

Before we start，let me provide some context to

my thoughts. Over the past century the world's economic growth has come in the main from OECD countries, and has benefited around a billion people. For the current century this will change. We are already seeing billions of people in the emerging markets starting to benefit from dramatic growth in their countries. The UN's millennium target of reducing by half the number of people living in extreme poverty has been achieved. Energy is fundamental to this journey of progress and development and, whether we like it or not, this means that the world will need more energy, not less.

论述之前做好背景介绍，世界领域内的大背景是经济突飞猛进，对能源的需求与日俱增，能源业面临的挑战也日益凸显，因而讨论本论题是有重要的实际意义的。

So far the industry has been able to rise to that challenge. For example, in the last 30 years, when oil consumption has grown by more than 40%, more oil has been found than the world has consumed. However we need to have a realistic and open debate on energy. We need to establish a common ground for discussion. We can't pretend, for example, that climate change is not a serious issue. Neither can we pretend that renewables are the only solution.

用具体的数据来表明能源业应对挑战的举措，“however”转折引出问题：能源消耗增大引起的气候变化问题，因此需要用更可持续的方式来利用能源。

> In seeking to set out a basis for addressing these issues, I will focus on three questions: What is the energy challenge? What should be the policy response? And what should be the business response?

背景叙述清楚之后，听众头脑中已经建立起大概的框架，立即进入正题。三个问题简洁明了地揭示要讨论的主题，引起听众的好奇和思考，吸引听众跟随报告人的讲解去追寻答案。

> The energy challenge has three dimensions: sufficiency, security and sustainability.

回答第一个问题：何谓能源挑战？包含三个方面：需求、安全和可持续。下文以此解释三个概念，层次清晰。

> Sufficiency is about demand. BP's projection is that the world's GDP will grow 80% in the next 20 years, and as a result we believe that energy demand will grow some 40% until 2030. This equates to two times the United States' current energy consumption — in addition to what the world uses today. 95% of that extra demand will come from the emerging markets, led by China and India. Our figure of 40% more energy is based on likely trends

in demand, supply, policy and technology. It's a projection, not a proposition. It is simply what we believe is most likely to happen. So the first part of the challenge is to supply enough energy to meet demand.

对听众可能会有疑问的专业术语进行释义，sufficiency 指的就是需求，同时摆出具体数据，加深听众的直观印象。

Second, when we look at demand and supply, there is a mismatch. For example, the US and China each use twice, as much oil as they produce; Russia produces three times as much as it uses. Six countries produce half the world's oil; three countries produce half the world's gas. It is easy to understand why governments worry about the reliability of supplies. So the second part of the energy challenge is security.

用举例和对比来说明能源供求关系，美国和中国“求”远大于“供”，而俄罗斯恰恰相反。能源分布和供求的不均衡势必会导致能源安全问题。

The third is sustainability. Put simply, an increase in energy demand of 40% is likely to result in an increase of over 25% in greenhouse gas emissions. We must find ways to supply energy on the scale required while minimizing environmental effects and without depleting critical resources such as water.

对复杂概念“sustainability”进行释义，“put simply”，简而言之，用数据摆一摆听众自然就明白了。

So what is the response to this three-dimensional challenge? Many have a part to play in this, from experts in academia to policy makers and businesses.

解决了第一个问题“能源挑战是什么”，转入第二个问题：在决策上如何应对？决策者（policy-maker）和行业领袖（business leaders）分别承担相应的责任：决策者建立框架，行业在此框架内提供产品和服务。

As I see it, policy-makers provide a framework. Businesses provide goods and services within that framework. Responsible business leaders want to make companies a force for good. But they also have to compete to survive. If governments want business to rise to a particular challenge and there is no obvious business case, they need to set conditions to make it happen. This is not an easy task for policy makers. They must and do think long term—indeed very long term. However they serve governments who are elected on short-term cycles. This is another mismatch. Businesses, particularly in the energy industry, also work on long-term cycles, often over decades.

照应前文中提到的能源危机的三个方面，政策框架必须对应解决这三个问题，如下文所示：

A Framework for Sufficiency and Security

Let us now apply this to energy sufficiency. In order to incentivize companies to produce energy, governments need to promoze competition and innovation. A great example is the shale oil and gas revolution that has led the US to the fastest growth in oil production outside OPEC. This was encouraged by a policy framework supportive of open competition, market prices and research and development. The same policy framework of competition and open access encouraged BP to invest in the seismic technology needed to find deep water oil and gas fields. Those developments have been game-changing for energy security. US oil production today is the highest for twenty years. Domestic natural gas could last up to 100 years. As a result energy imports have fallen dramatically.

解决需求和安全问题的政策框架是鼓励公开竞争、市场定价和研发。报告人用例证法支撑论点：美国利用页岩油气一跃成为 OPEC 之外石油生产增长最快的国家。

A Framework for Sustainability

Looking at sustainability, the picture is more complicated. The market does not always deliver the best outcome for society. But policy can harness market forces positively.

如何保证可持续性是个更加复杂的问题，报告人从低碳能源、能源运输、可再生能源等各方面进行论述，运用摆数据、举例子、作对比等方法，力求把复杂问题说清说透。最后阐明BP集团对减排政策的立场态度：

We support action by governments, individually and collectively.

For sustainable energy, two things are critical: saving energy through efficiency; and switching energy to lower carbon sources. Energy efficiency needs to be addressed in a fundamental way. In its journey through production, conversion, transmission and final use, the vast majority of energy is lost, mainly as waste heat. Academic studies suggest these losses could be more than 80%. The potential for efficiency improvements is huge. It would reduce costs and emissions, and tackle sufficiency, security and sustainability.

When it comes to switching energy, governments can and must act in various ways to encourage energy efficiency or low-carbon energy. It must start with setting a price on carbon and BP's preference is to harness the market: through cap and trade systems; through regulations, such as the US CAFE standards; through targets, such as for biofuls; or through direct support, such as tax credits for wind power.

On that last example: in 1998 the US Government projected that the US would have 4 GW of wind capacity by 2020. But policy support encouraged business investment, and this year wind capacity reached over 51 GW, literally off the chart of the forecast. In deciding how to act, it makes sense to look at where the biggest issues are. Coal is the world's biggest source of emissions today due to its widespread use in power generation. Natural gas is the fastest-growing fossil fuel, and it is the cleanest, with half the emissions of conventional coal. Shifting from coal to natural gas is probably the most important action to reduce emissions in the medium term. As an example CO_2 emissions in the US last year fell by nearly 2%. Switching to gas in power plants was a clear contributing factor.

Let's turn to transport; here oil is the primary fuel.

Tough emissions targets have been set. In addition, the potential to improve energy efficiency in combustion engines is significant. BP expects it to double in the next 20 years, partly as a result of regulations like CAFE. Through more efficient vehicles and increased biofuls substitution, oil consumption has now peaked in the OECD world. But will it continue to grow in emerging markets. We expect global oil demand to grow 20% to 2030, less than 1% a year. That said, existing fields globally show a natural decline of some 4% a year, corresponding to half of Saudi Arabia's annual production. So there is a constant need to use technology to increase yields in existing fields, and to find new reservoirs at new frontiers. The bottom line is that, in our most likely scenario, fossil fuels will still account for some 80% of the total energy mix in 2030. Even in the most radical scenario from the International Energy Agency, the so-called 450 scenario—fossil fuels, remain the major source of energy.

Non-fossil energy — renewables, nuclear and hydro—is set to grow faster than any single fossil fuel, but from such a low base that in the medium term it cannot turn the dial that much compared with efficiency and switching from coal to gas. We expect that renewables at best will reach 6-7% of the mix by 2030. Fossil fuels per se are not incompatible with a healthy planet. It is about the mix; and it is about energy efficiency.

BP's position on this is clear: We support

action by governments, individually and collectively, to limit emissions; We believe the best way to limit emissions is to price carbon on as wide a scale as possible in order to stimulate efficiency and innovation; We also support transitional incentives to help emerging low-carbon options become commercial at scale.

决策者层面叙述清楚后，转入行业角度，作为能源企业该如何应对？从 BP 集团的实际情况出发，阐明应对举措：掌握行业前沿技术、加强安全管理、更有效地发挥董事会的作用等。

The Business Response

So that is our thinking on policy, but what is our response as businesses? As an energy industry, we are at an inflection point, with many doors opening at once. The shale revolution has transformed the US and it is spreading. In the deepwater, we are finding hydrocarbons at unprecedented pressures and temperatures. New enhanced oil recovery techniques are giving many depleted reservoirs a second life. And new possibilities are emerging in low-carbon fuels and energy efficiency, from cellulosic biofuels to new generations of hybrid cars. The industry is broadening—to provide more energy—and it is also deepening—by working in more specialized areas.

The New Super-Major

This poses big questions for companies such as BP—so-called "super-majors" —who have operated everywhere from the reservoir to the pump. The global reach of the super-majors was seen as strength, with the ability to replicate successful projects again and again round the world. These old certainties no longer apply. The world is changing. We have seen the rise of the National Oil Companies, the NOCs. These NOCs are becoming more capable, both at home and abroad. In the early 70s the largest international oil companies produced more than 50% of the world's oil; today's super-majors produce just 10%.

Our role has evolved. Our view is that in a broader and deeper industry, a super-major can't be super at everything. It needs to make choices. Where once the super-major was defined by scale the super-major of the future will be defined by quality-deep capability, applied to specific areas of activity.

BP's Response

For BP this is a natural progression. We had to develop specialisms to survive after the nationalizations in the 70s. We developed new skills at the frontiers of the industry, in the deep water and giant fields of the North Sea and the Gulf of Mexico, as well as the Arctic conditions of

Alaska. And then in 2010 we experienced a defining event with the Deepwater Horizon accident. We deeply regret this incident and the eleven lives that were lost. To date, we have spent nearly ＄15 billion in operational response and clean-up costs and more than ＄8 billion in claims to individuals, businesses and government entities. And our task is not yet finished.

We also committed ourselves to learning, applying and sharing the lessons we have learned from the accident with industry, government and regulators around the world. We aim to emerge a safer, stronger BP that creates shareholder value in a sustainable way. We also remain committed to the US and to our role in its energy industry. But our response is more than just in the development of our skills and specialisms. We have understood the challenge that I set out earlier. We see the role of the policymakers and the limitations that are placed on them. We see the rise of the NOCs. Just as our role is changing as a super-major so is the way in which Boards need to operate. Whether I am chairing a Board in Britain or in Sweden, the conversations are the same.

We have seen the challenges from the financial and the banking crisis. We have seen the concerns that have been voiced around the world about the role of companies and indeed the role of business. I truly believe that business is a force for good in the world, conducted in a way which meets the expectations of shareholders and society at large. But business needs to build the most valuable asset, which is trust: trust from shareholders that we can create value; as well as from society that we can operate safely now and in the long term. We need to be responsible to our shareholders, but responsive to the expectations of those with whom we come into contact through our activities.

I have led public corporations for two decades. Again and again I have found that trust is the critical underpinning of all achievements. Also, Boards operate differently in different jurisdictions. In the UK and US shareholder value is in focus. In the UK there was a debate about 10 years ago whether Boards were responsible to shareholders only, or to the broader stakeholder community. The UK came up with the notion of "enlightened shareholder value" as a way to recognise societal concerns. It was in line with the concept of responsibility and responsiveness that I mentioned earlier. In continental Europe and certainly in Sweden the balance of the interests between companies, government, shareholders and society has been in stronger focus for quite some time. But whichever system is used, the modern Board of a global company has to work in a way that allows it to do the things that only the Board can do.

Let us be clear: the Board does not manage the company; it governs the company. These are two very different activities. Boards need to organise themselves so they can govern in a way:

That makes sure that the company has the right strategy;

That understands the risks to the company and how they are being mitigated;

That has oversight of the performance of the Company and the executive team.

And above all that, it has to have the time to understand the challenges facing the company not in the short-term but in the long-term. And it must set the tone from the top which ensures that the company is a good citizen in the societies in which it works. For companies like BP and Volvo it means understanding the energy challenge and recognizing the very real role that those companies can play in working with policy makers and society to develop the right solutions.

So, let me leave you with 6 messages:

结尾部分，言简意赅地总结全文观点。

Energy benefits society. And demand will rise with economic growth;

There is a geographical mismatch between demand and supply that will continue to create geopolitical tension;

The world will continue to be largely dependent on fossil fuel in the medium term, and we need to go to new frontiers to secure supply;

We can mitigate the environmental effects from fossil fuels through improved energy efficiency and by switching from coal to gas;

We must continue research and development for renewables to make sure that we can provide the world with energy solutions also in the longer term;

Business can be the glue that can tie all of this together, but it must have the trust of society to do so.

Beneath these simple statements lie a host of complex questions. The policy tools, resources, technologies and investment exist to address the energy challenge. I am optimistic that we can provide energy that is sufficient, secure and sustainable into the future. I look forward to discussing them now.

提出后续需要跟进研究和讨论的问题，并再次点题，同时表明自己对行业前景的看法：对未来能源的供给、安全、可持续持乐观态度。

So over to you. Thank you.

简洁明了的结束语和致谢，毫不拖泥带水。

第二章　商务谈判

谈判是人与人之间，为了达成某种利益而进行的交流，它广泛存在于社会生活的各个层面，如租客与房东之间、老板和员工之间、买主与摊贩之间、孩子与家长之间。租客们为了更低的房租、员工们为了更好的福利、买主为了便宜的菜价、孩子为了更多的玩具而和房东、老板、摊贩、家长之间的讨价还价都属于谈判的范畴。在当今社会，商务活动越来越多，商务交流越来越频繁，不同利益方之间的商务谈判也成为一种重要的谈判形式。

商务谈判是建立在人们需要的基础之上，谈判双方或多方为了达成某些经济利益而进行协商的行为，合作与竞争共存于商务谈判的整个过程。它主要集中在经济领域，其目的是解决利益冲突，满足贸易需求。

商务谈判需要具备谈判主体（双方人员）、谈判客体（议题或标的）和谈判目的三个基本要素，能否顺利开启还需要看双方是否共同有解决问题的良好愿望、是否在为谈判成功做出努力。

商务谈判有书面形式和口头形式两种。口头谈判有利于谈判各方当面提出条件和意见，互相能够更直接、更有效地做出回应，如面对面谈判和电话谈判。这种形式时效性强但决策风险大，需要成熟的谈判技巧；书面谈判可以使谈判各方对于要协商的问题有更充足的考虑时间，如函电谈判。这种形式的谈判不用承受面面相对的压力，但由于不能通过肢体动作或面部表情判定对方对于某一问题的反应，它更需要在文字表达时用词要精准，避免因词不达意引起的不必要的争议。

根据不同的标准，商务谈判有不同的划分类别。按谈判范围划分，有国际商务谈判和国内商务谈判；按谈判地点划分，有主场谈判、客场谈判和中立地谈判；按谈判参与人数划分，有单人谈判、小组谈判和大型谈判；除此之外，还有按谈判内容划分、按谈判性质划分、按谈判时的态度划分等方式。

商务谈判的特征：第一，商务谈判的核心点是经济利益，其本质是经济利益的得失；第二，谈判的对象有不确定性，可自由结合，自由选择；第三，谈判的内容要具体，明确。

商务谈判的原则：第一，遵纪守法，任何协议的签署都需要在符合法律规定的前提下进行，违反法规的协议或合同没有法律效力，其规定的权利不受法律的保护，义务也得不到有效的监督。国内商务谈判要遵守本国的法律法规，国际商务谈判不仅要遵守双方国家的有关法规，还要熟悉国际经济法和相关的国际惯例。无论口头形式的谈判还是书面形式的谈判都要法律化，所有语言、文字的形成都要以法律为准绳，否则，一切都是徒劳。第二，平等互利，成功的谈判不但要追求己方的最大利益，也能维护对方的合法权利，得到双赢的结果。谈判的目的虽然是己方利益的最大化，但谈判过程中只片面坚持己方的立场不能达成有效、友好的协议。谈判的顺利进行需要各方的相互配合，对各方的利益都有所顾及，形成双赢或多赢的局面是最令人满意的谈判结果。第三，诚实信用，诚实守信不是说把己方的谈判目的、谈判底线和盘托出，而是要求双方的出发点要诚挚，真正为解决实际问题。不仅在谈判中要言行一致，结束谈判后也要遵守承诺，积极履行协议的条款。

成功的商务谈判一般会按照 APRAM 的模式逐步开展：

项目评估（appraisal）：在正式谈判开始之前，先要对谈判项目进行整体分析，判断项目的可行性，确定己方要达到的目标并估测对方的谈判目标。

制定谈判计划（planning）：根据双方的谈判目的，制定详细的时间计划、人员计划、预算计划和策略计划。

建立关系（relationship）：要努力表示己方的诚意，坦诚地面对对方提出的问题，争取得到对方的信任。言必行，行必果。

达成协议（agreement）：对意见一致的问题，双方进行确认；对意见不同的问题，双方继续协商、交换意见，努力寻求双赢的解决方案。

协议的履行和关系的维持（maintenance）：己方要信守承诺，履行协议，对对方的配合要给予积极的回应；谈判后依然与对方保持接触，对对方保持关注。

商务谈判按照其进行过程，大致可分为开局阶段（opening stage）、报价阶段（offer stage）、磋商阶段（counter-offer stage）和成交阶段（transaction concluding stage）。

一、商务谈判的开局阶段

我们常说“万事开头难”，“良好的开端是成功的一半”，这种说法也同样适用于商务谈判。在开局阶段，谈判双方彼此熟悉，开始真正的交流和沟通，初步讨论谈判的前期事务如谈判的目标、内容、进度等非实质性问题，并在此基础上就谈判内容双方分别发表陈述。谈判过程中，开局的顺利进行可以为之后具体内容的谈判铺平道路。谈判双方在开局阶段这个过程持续时间不长，但对整个谈判过程有着重要的影响，起着一定的制约作用，所以谈判人员对此要高度重视。谈判开局阶段的主要工作是营造良好的气氛，做好开场陈述。

(一) 营造良好的气氛

谈判气氛是指谈判双方通过各自所表现的态度、作风而建立起来的谈判环境。谈判气氛的形成和变化对谈判的成败得失有至关重要的影响，关系到整个谈判的根本利益和前途。因此，富有专业经验的谈判人员会在谈判开局阶段争取创造和谐的谈判气氛，为谈判的成功铺平道路。

1. 礼貌尊重（be polite and respectful）。

首先要准时。高层领导的出席可以表现出对谈判的重视和诚意。谈判人员服饰仪表干净整洁，男性着装要成熟稳重，女性则突出端庄柔美；行为举止大方得体，精力充沛；言语谦和有礼，语速适中。例如：

May I present Mr. X, the general manager of our department?

Please allow me to introduce Mr. X.

It is a privilege to know Mr. X.

作相互介绍时，一般的顺序是把年轻的、地位稍低的人介绍给年长的、头衔高的人；把己方的人介绍给对方的人；把男性介绍给女性。

2. 自然轻松（be natural and relaxed）。

不宜过早地对谈判的实质内容进行讨论。在开局阶段，谈判双方或各方还处于比较紧张的情绪中，热情的握手和微笑，自然亲切的寒暄如私人问候，轻松的日常话题如各自的经历（personal experience）、体育新闻（sports news）等可以舒缓双方或各方的心理压力，但切忌谈论政治或宗教等敏感话题。例如：

How is your journey? Did you have a good rest?

Would anyone like something to drink before we begin?

Did you watch the World Cup last night? Which team do you support?

3. 友好合作（be friendly and cooperative）。

谈判者要真诚地表达对对方的友好愿望和对合作成功的期望。要表现出对谈判成功的信心。谈判过程中会有分歧，但相信最终能达到各方满意的结果。例如：

I wish the negotiation a complete success.

We hope we can reach an agreement after the negotiation.

We'll come out from this meeting as winners.

We sincerely hope this transaction will be successful and we can establish business partnership with you.

It is our hope that the result of the negotiation will make both parties satisfied.

在见面的最初几分钟内，谈判双方要竭力营造出良好的谈判气氛，但这种气氛可能随着谈判的实质磋商过程不断变化甚至恶化，所以谈判过程中要注意通过平等互利真诚合作的指导方针及具体措施来维护这种气氛。但是值得注意的是，谈判者除了要掌握建立良好谈判气氛的方法之外，还必须根据具体的谈判形势，己方所处的地位与环境，恰当地调节谈判的气氛。例如：

A：Hello， Mr. Wang， nice to see you again. How are you?

B：I'm good. How about you?

A：I'm OK， we just moved in our new house. Everything is in a great mess. It's a nightmare. But I'll appreciate not having to spend so much time commuting to my work every day.

B：Yes，it took me nearly one hour to get here today. Public transport service in this area is not so good.

A：Well，will you like a cup of coffee?

B：Thank you. And that would be nice.

A：So，how's business in your section?

B：Not too bad. We have a lot of work to do as we have signed a number of contracts with other companies.

A：Then I think you can say a few words about that first.

在上述对话例子中，两个谈判人员有过交往，并且关系不错。这是营造良好谈判气氛的一个积极因素。两人的谈判并没有单刀直入，而是先从日常话题谈起，聊到了两人都有共鸣的比较糟糕的交通问题。然后由表及里、由浅入深地循序渐进，慢慢开启谈判之门，使得谈判可以顺利展开。

4. 留心文化差异（be culture-awared）。

在言谈举止中，还要留意文化差异。例如：某中国石油公司谈判小组赴中东某国进行一项工程承包谈判。在闲聊中，中方的成员对中东盛行的伊斯兰教的评价引起了对方的不满。当谈及实质性问题时，对方较为激进的商务谈判人员丝毫不让步，并一再流露撤出谈判的意图。在此沟通过程中，中方负责商务条款的成员无意中评论了中东盛行的伊斯兰教，这就导致了文化冲突，致使对方成员不悦而不愿意与中方合作，为此中方谈判人员应该向对方成员道歉。可见，谈判人员在谈判前应该了解对方的习俗及喜好，避免类似情况的发生，正所谓知己知彼才能百战百胜。

（二）协商谈判议程

谈判议程就是关于谈判的主要议题、谈判的原则框架、议题的先后顺序与时间安排。谈判之初，一般应首先将谈判议程确定下来。谈判议程的商定，实质上也是谈判的内容，因为议程本身如何将会决定谈判者在以后的工作中是否有主动性，将会决定谈判的最终成果。

1. 明确谈判目标。

双方明确表述出来对此次谈判所期望达到的目的和意图，明确双方为什么要进行此次谈判。例如：

To begin with, we have to settle our disputes about the delivery of your supplied products.

2. 明确谈判计划及进度。

在整场谈判中，双方要涉及的议题及双方必须遵守的规程，确定洽谈事项的先后顺序及具体时间。以下例句可供参考：

How would you like to proceed with the negotiation? Do you have any plans?

Let's draw up a schedule for this negotiation, shall we?

We have worked out an agenda for our discussion. If you have any problem, please don't hesitate to let us know.

3. 确定谈判的场所、参与谈判的人员。

下面的对话完整地描述了协商谈判议程的过程：

A：So, thank you for coming, everyone. It's really honorable to see you all here. First of all, may I suggest you take a look at the agenda in front of you? Would you like to make any comment on that?

B：Yes, I wonder whether or not we can begin with the issue of shipment first. We really need to reach an agreement on that.

A：That's true, but it's really a complex issue. That's why I put it last. I thought it might be much better for us to start with the points we have in common. We'll then move to the shipment issue.

B：All right. That sounds reasonable.

A：Well, before we go any further, I would like to say I strongly feel that both of our two sides intend to come to an agreement today. The market is becoming more and more competitive and our combined strength will bring us more advantages, and lead us to a brighter future. Now, I think Richard would like to say a few words about that.

在这个对话中，A方通过让大家阅读派发的材料了解谈判安排，并简明扼要地说明了做这种安排的原因，让谈判双方都明白了谈判的进程，并表达了对谈判结果的乐观预期。

（三）开场陈述

开场陈述是指谈判双方就本次洽谈的内容，陈述各自的观点、立场及其建议。开场陈述是依次进行，重点是陈述己方的利益需求，多采用横向铺开的陈述方法，而不会对某个问题进行深入细致的分析。表达形式包括书面形式、口头形式以及书面表达并做口头补充三种。陈述的内容一般包括以下几点：

• 己方的利益以及首要利益。

• 己方对谈判问题的理解。

• 己方对对方建议的各项回答。

• 己方的原则及为达到共同利益可做的让步。

开场陈述是谈判开局阶段的正式发言，对谈判气氛有着直接的影响。因此，谈判人员应对开场陈述给予高度的重视，做出充分的准备工作，在此过程中做到把握要点、镇定自若、留有余地，具体表现为：

• 言简意赅表达己方的意图，不要漫无边际地东拉西扯。简洁为贵。

• 不要阐述双方的共同利益，以免造成对方的误会。更不要对对方的利益妄加猜测，导致谈判破裂。

• 顾全大局，着眼全盘，不要只看眼前利益，不要把精力只集中于一个问题。

• 维护自己的权利，不要忙于自己承担义务。

• 喜怒不行于色，听到不利于己方的表达时不要急于反驳，镇定自若。

• 要随时纠正对方的某些概念性错误。

例如，A公司是一家实力雄厚的石油公司，为了提高开采效率，需要大量采购B公司所生产的极其先进的石油开采设备。而B公司正想通过销售这批设备给A公司来打开其在A公司所在国的市场。于是，双方精选了久经沙场的谈判干将，就设备购买价格和运输方式展开磋商。

Statement of A: The equipment of your company is attractive to us. We intend to replace our traditional oil field equipment with your efficient ones. The key issue now is time, we should reach an agreement on the issues of time and delivery as soon as possible. We have no contact before but we heard you are quite cooperative. This is what we want to say, is that clear?

Statement of B: We are pleased to sell the equipment to your company. By adopting high technology, its field efficiency is much better than that of others. It is well-received on the market abroad, so there is not much left over. What we are concerned is the quantity you will choose. This is our attitude, is that clear?

上述双方在陈述中都开门见山地表明了自己的意图，这就会使双方在之后的实质磋商阶段有了明确的谈判方向。双方在此阶段都没有提及共同利益，更没有对彼此的利益进行猜测。

当双方陈述完各自的利益、要求之后，为了达到双方的共同利益就需要提出倡议。所谓倡议是指一种能把双方互提建设性意见，使得谈判向着有利于双方的结果进行下去。倡议应注意的几点：

互提建议时要使建议具有可行性，直截了当、简单明了、切忌拐弯抹角。比如：

A：Now，do you have any new ideas?

B：We may reach an agreement on price by adjusting the delivery conditions.

双方互提意见，有来有往。切忌一方滔滔不绝，令对方感到厌烦。比如：

A：Do you have any suggestions for what to discuss?

B：We wonder if ...

不要过多地为己方的建议辩护，过多地对对方的建议抨击，以免引起对方的反感甚至恶化成敌意，不利于谈判的顺利进行。

二、商务谈判的报价阶段

商务谈判的核心就是经济利益，价格的谈判是整个谈判过程中的一个重要部分，针对价格的谈判主要集中在报价阶段和之后的磋商阶段。合理的报价和平等的协商往往能够对谈判的成功起决定性作用，而很多谈判的失败恰恰就是由于在价格问题上没有达成一致的观点。在本节中，我们会讨论如何报价，不同报价顺序的利弊以及在报价阶段经常会用到的一些英语表达方式。

（一）报价前的准备

1. 报价前需要了解的问题。

商务谈判中对产品的报价并不是凭空而来，而是在综合考虑了自己产品的质量及成本、市场行情以及谈判对手的情况之后向对方提出的价格。在谈判中，一方向另一方报价时，不光要考虑到自己的利润，还要考虑到对方的接受程度。报价太高，会被对方认为没有表现出谈判的诚意；而报价太低，会使自己的利润打折扣。所以在报价之前，要对自己的产品价位、主要目标市场及同行产品报价比较了解，然后尽可能多方面先了解客户情况，做到知己知彼。

首先，认真分析客户的购买意愿，掌握他们的真正需求，例如对一款空气压缩机报价之前，要对下列问题有所了解：

这款机器对方是用在哪方面的，与什么设备配套使用？功率有多大？输入输出电压是多少？要多少台？要不要税，是哪种税？交货期有什么要求？

What kind of equipment does the machine have to be interfaced with?

What is the power of it?

What is the input voltage? And the output voltage?

What's the total amount of your order?

What other requirements for the machine do

you have?

有时候需要到现场察看，要了解使用的设备的详细数据等等。然后再决定进行尝试性报价或正式报价。

其次，了解主要竞争对手，做好市场跟踪调研，清楚市场的最新动态。比较有实力的外商一般在中国大陆或香港有办事处，对中国的市场行情很了解。由于市场信息透明度高，市场价格变化更加迅速，因此，报价要随行就市。

2. 关于报价应有的概念。

• 报价的基本原则（basic principle）：报价时我们既要考虑到己方的合理利润，又要考虑该报价被接受的可能性，两者的最佳结合点即为最理想的报价。

• 报价的上下限（upper and lower limits）：从谈判中卖方的角度来看，报价的下限是成本价格，上限是对方的购买力。

• 报价的形式（forms of offer）：口头报价和书面报价。书面报价白纸黑字，约束力强；口头报价比较灵活，但难以描述清楚比较复杂的数字、图表。在实际操作中，常以书面报价为主，口头报价为辅。

• 报价的时机（best time to offer）：报价的最佳时机出现在对方的询价之后。在价格谈判中，避免过早地提到价格问题，要巧妙地回避价格的讨论。通过展示自己产品的优点、未来发展以及该产品可为对方带来的实际利益等来吸引对方对产品的兴趣，使对方的焦点集中在产品的实用性上。当对方表达出购买的欲望，开始询价时再进行报价容易达到事半功倍的效果。可以用以下句式来唤起对方对产品的兴趣：

If you try it out, I'm sure you'll find that this product deserves your investment.

Through a comprehensive comparison, you can see that our product has the edge over other ones.

You may trust me that any money spent now will bring you big profits in future.

• 报价的起点（the starting point）：谨慎对待第一个数字：第一个数字最关键，卖方开高价有利，买方出底价有利。其原因在于：

作为卖方，报的开盘价决定了此次谈判可能成交的最高价格。在报出开盘价后，卖方不能再报出更高的价格，对方会在开盘价的基础上不断压价，而不会接受比开盘价更高的价格。此外，高的报价可以使卖方在谈判过程中有让步的余地，使谈判过程有伸缩性。

作为买方，所报的开盘价决定了可能成交的最低价格。进一步开出低于开盘价会显得出尔反尔，没有诚意，卖方也不会接受。

（二）报价的策略

1. 报价差别策略。

在谈判之前，要尽可能多地了解对方，看对方公司所在地是否属于你们的目标市场、对方的经营范围、购买能力、对此类产品的熟悉程度等，然后有针对性地进行报价，也就是“个性化报价”。

如果对方对此类产品的成本、性能、市场行情非常熟悉，并且想建立长期业务联系，那么报价时要接近底价以表达诚意，并和市场上其他同类产品进行对比，突出自己的优点，强调其他产品的缺点来吸引对方，达到塑造自己产品价值的目的。例如：

You are an expert in this field. You know quite well that our products enjoy high popularity in Asian market for their reliability. They are energy-saving, easy to learn and easy to operate. Besides that, their price is more competitive than that of German machines. they are far better in so many aspects. We want to set up a long term business relationship with you, so we will offer you the best price, that is , XX for each piece.

如果谈判对方不是此类产品的行家，那么可以多介绍产品的用途、优点及未来的发展，价格可适当报高一点。

2. 报价顺序策略。

关于谈判双方谁先报价的问题，没有明确规定。但按惯例来说，发起谈判者应该先报价；卖方与买方之间一般是卖方先报价。

先报价有利也有弊。它的好处在于己方可以提出期望的价位，为价格谈判划定了一个基准线，使最后的成交价不会偏离自己的心理价位太远。它的弊端就是使己方暴露在明处，即使对方对报价满意也不会表现出来，更不会泄露他们的价格，而是调整计划，集中力量压低报价，获得意料外的利益。

后报价的利弊与之相反。好处就是可以身在暗处，根据对方的报价及时调整谈判策略，弊端就是谈判需要在对方圈定的范围内进行，受对方影响和制约。比如某件商品一方报价5000元，另一方不可能压价到几百元。

那么，到底如何利用报价顺序来为己方获取更多利益呢？

先报价更有利的情况：竞争比较激烈，谈判气氛紧张，这时先报价可以推进谈判进行，力争牵制对方；或己方做了充分的准备工作，对产品和谈判对手有深入的了解，这时可以先行报价来先发制人、约束对方。

后报价更有利的情况：对方对此类产品及市场非常熟悉，而己方是个外行，这时就要有耐心、后报价，从对方的报价中获得信息来调整己方的计划。

而当双方是关系友好的合作伙伴，或双方都对此产品了解颇多时，先报价和后报价就没有实质区别了。

3. 报价分割策略。

有些产品是按“盒”、“箱”等单位出售，但如果一箱的价格比较高，我们可以报出平均单位内相应的价格。此种报价策略是能够迎合对方的求廉心理，使客户在第一时间能够接受。例如：

The price of the product is X. But it can be used for 1 year, so it only costs you X each day. It's really reasonable for you to own it.

4. 资源整合策略。

整体报价不变，但将产品的价值、功能重新整合，例如突出周全的配套服务项目，比如建立了免费咨询服务（free consultation）、送货上门（home delivery）、安装调试（installation）、终身保修（lifetime warranty）等一套比较完善的售后服务机制，给客户实惠的感觉。

（三）报价的实施

经过报价之前的周密分析、充分准备之后，在报价时无论采用口头形式或书面形式，都有表达清晰准确，不拖泥带水。口头报价时可将要点写到纸上，避免出现差错。

报价时的态度要坚定果断，犹豫不定是大忌。

报价之后不要主动进行解释和说明。因为无论报价高低，对方都会进行猜疑；当对方要求对报价进行解释时，应遵循的原则是：不问不答，有问必答，避虚就实，能言不书。报价时的常用句式：

We can offer you a quotation based on the X market. Our offers are firm for 3 days.

We offer you our best prices, at which we have done a lot of business with other customers.

We are willing to make you a firm offer at this price.

要求对方报价时可用的句式：

Could you offer us the price of X?

What is your quotation of X?

What is your F. O. B. Prices? And what is your price on C. I. F. basis?

三、商务谈判的磋商阶段

一般情况下，报价方报出开盘价后，另一方不会立即接受，而是要求对方开出更优惠、更实在的价格，这时双方的谈判进入了价格磋商阶段，也就是我们通常所说的讨价还价。报价的高低框定了价格谈判的大致范围，而讨价还价则会直接影响价格的最终确定，这恰恰就是谈判能否成功的导火索。磋商阶段是商务谈判的核心阶段，其往往也是谈判气氛最紧张的阶段。在此我们将讨论讨价还价的技巧并介绍相关的英语句型。

（一）讨价

讨价就是报价方报价并进行价格解释后，己方在价格评论的基础上要求对方更改报价的行为。讨价的原因有很多，比如报价不在自己的心理预期内，或报价符合期望目标但通过讨价进一步压低对方价格，为己方赢得更多的利益空间等。

1. 关于讨价应有的概念。

• 如何讨价：讨价是伴随着己方的价格评论或评价进行的，己方的价格评论为讨价的顺利进行提供了具体的支持性依据。在首次讨价时的价格评价可以宏观地谈己方对对方报价的态度。如果对方更改了报价，应该再次针对新的报价进行价格评价以便己方进行新一轮的讨价。进行价格评论可用的句型：

Everyone knows, the price of crude oil has greatly decreased, so your offer is unacceptable.

It was a higher price than that offered by other suppliers.

It's very obvious that your offer is beyond our expectation and we don't find it competitive at all.

We think that other offers compare favorably with the quotations we get here.

• 讨价的程序：第一步是整体讨价（general bargaining）。整体讨价也被称为笼统讨价，即在第一次针对报价方的总体价格进行讨价时，可从全局着手，要求报价方从整体上改善价格。例如：

We can't accept your offer unless the offer is renewed.

To have this business concluded, you need to adjust your offer to a lower one.

第二步是具体讨价（specific bargaining）。具体讨价常用于整体报价后。整体报价结束后，己方仍对部分项目报价不满意，这时要求报价方针对具体报价内容分项报价。具体报价要有针对性，要将具体的讨论内容准确划分成几块，逐一讨价。成功的具体讨价的规律：首先从最不合理、水分最大的部分开始，其次是虚头中等部分，最后是水分最小的部分。如：

现在原材料价格下降得厉害，成品肯定还能再降点价。另外，在付款方式上，我们不能接受即时信用证，但可以用承兑交单的方式。

Since the prices of raw materials have been decreased, I think you should adjust the prices of the products accordingly. Besides that, for the terms of payment, we could accept to pay by D/A, but not a L/C.

第三步是新一轮讨价（next-round bargaining）。在整体讨价和具体讨价之后，报价方所改善的报价可能仍然不是己方的理想目标。这时就要重新开始新一轮的讨价，继续向对方提出整体讨价的要求，进而具体讨价。例如：

We want to place a large order with you. So could you consider again to give us a really special offer?

• 讨价的次数：讨价的次数不是固定的数字，讨价的次数服从于讨价的目的，同时也受心理因素的限制。一般来说，当对方首次报价后，先要进行一次整体讨价；然后再针对具体每一部分至少应讨价一次，在对方就该部分改善要价后再往下进行，否则宁可原地不动，继续讨价，直到达到讨价的目的为止。

• 讨价的策略：在谈判过程中，太过直率和坦白、"一步到位"的讨价会降低报价方的心理满足程度，降低了最终成交的可能性；而有技巧、有策略的讨价不仅会最大限度地满足自己的需求，也能使对方从心理上认同、接纳己方，给对方更多的心理满足。这有利于营造轻松的谈判氛围，有利于促进和加强双方进一步的合作关系。

• 投石问路策略：在谈判场上掌握了主动权，就有更大的可能使谈判结果向己方倾斜。那么如何做到这一点呢？这就需要从多方面了解谈判对手，除了谈判前的资料收集，在谈判时也要尽可能多地去探询到对方对己方某一行为的反应和对策，这就是谈判中的投石问路策略。在对方报价后，己方不急于还价，而是提出种种假设条件下的价格问题，以试探对方的虚实。例如：

If we sign a contract with you for 3 years,

what's the discount you can offer?

Is there any difference if we pay by cash or by installments?

If we can offer the material to you, then what's the price of the finished product?

一般来讲，这种基于事实的假设性提问使对方难以拒绝，所以这种策略能够帮助己方刺探到对方的商业习惯，进一步接近对方的底牌。如果己方是报价方，那么在应对这种策略时，可以根据对方的问题估测他们的购买力。接到对方的“石头”后立即回敬过去。例如：

对方：If we increase our order to X, what's your price?

回复：That depends on whether you place the order right now.

• 挑剔策略：挑剔策略是谈判双方都可使用的策略。买方可以对卖方的产品严格要求，对具体细节仔细检查，挑毛病、找岔子并以此为依据要求对方调整价格。卖方也可以向买方提出问题、加以指责以削弱对方讨价的力度。

（二）还价

还价在对方报价、己方讨价之后，根据估算的对方低价和己方的理想价格，主动地或是应对方要求而提出自己的价格条件。还价的成功可以使对方接受自己的预期价格，使自己的利益得到保证。

1. 关于还价应有的概念。

•还价前的准备：进行充分的讨价；估测对方的低价。

•还价的起点：还价可以分多次进行，还价的起点是指第一次还价的价格。还价的起点对谈判双方的赢利空间有直接的影响。还价和报价一样不能言而无据、信口开河。还价太高会使自己的利益缩水，还价太低又显得没有诚意，令对方不能接受甚至失去谈判的兴趣，不利于谈判的进行。总之，还价起点的确定，不可凭主观想象或某个因素来进行，而应该综合考虑，以确保还价起点的成功。还价起点受三个因素的制约：买方理想成交价（expected price），产品的成本价（cost price），还价次数（times of counter-offer）。

理论上来说，还价起点的下限是产品成本价，上限是买方的理想成交价。在此范围内，还价起点要尽可能地低。原因在于，一方面，这样能给报价方施压，改变对方的判断，扩大自己的利益空间。另一方面，首次还价就能够得到报价方认可的可能性很小，利用较低的还价起点和还价次数制造合理的“还价台阶”，为之后的还价留有余地。

•还价的方式：按还价的依据来分，还价方式有按比价还价和按成本价还换。按还价的项目来分，还价方式有总体还价和具体还价。

2. 还价策略。

•恰当利用还价时机：还价时机选择得当可以减少还价次数，改善还价效果，因此还价时机是谈判者十分重视的问题。首次还价应在报价方对讨价做出回应并改善报价后进行，其最佳时机是在报价人对报价作了两次改善之后。例如：

You have lowered the offer by 3%, but it is

still hard for us to accept the price. So we hope you can reduce 5% on the basis of the original quotation.

We have seen the effort you have made for the deal, and to show our sincerity, we will make a counter-offer to you of ＄150 per ton F. O. B. New York.

• "长线"策略：以站在对方角度考虑问题的方式，向对方灌输如能成交对方将得到的利益，确认给对方的好处。畅想本次合作成功后双方的发展前景，强调双方的长远目标以将对方的注意力转移，使对方对己方的还价放松警惕。例如：

We really want to set up a long-term business relationship with you. If you can accept the counter-offer, then more orders will follow.

• "最后通牒"策略：即将最终还价告知报价方。一般情况下，当买方在谈判中处于有利地位或者买方已经无力再提高还价时会亮出最终还价。虽然是最终还价，但买方仍然要注意措辞，言语不能太犀利。例如：

This is the final counter-back. If you can't accept it, then we have nothing to talk about.

This is the highest price for us. Otherwise we can only call the deal off.

在这两句话中，买方都用了强势、坚决的态度，这很有可能会僵化谈判气氛，使谈判朝着不利的方向发展。"最后通牒"

策略的使用是为了达成交易，所以，发出最后通牒时用比较和缓的态度，说话内容留有余地往往能达到最终目的。例如：

您说的完全有道理，可惜我们只能开出这样的条件，您看能否通融一下？

What you have said is reasonable, but this is really the upper limit we can offer, so could you make an exception in our favor?

Please consider our final price, X yuan for one piece, or we can offer you a commission of 2% at most, otherwise we may turn to other suppliers.

（三）让步

在价格谈判中，如果在讨价还价后双方仍存在利益冲突，为了谈判继续进行以达成最后的交易，双方都要做出让步。如何以己方较小的让步来换取对方较大的让步是需要技巧的，在本节中我们将会探讨让步的策略。

1. 关于让步的一些概念。

• 让步的表现形式：卖方价格的不断递减与买方价格的不断递升。

• 让步的时机：商务谈判中让步的实质是以退为进，牺牲小利益换取大回报。让步不能主观臆断、随意进行，轻而易举的让步会导致己方的让步失去价值，非但不能使对方获得心理上的满足，为自己赢得利益，反而很有可能使对方认为让步有诈或者使对方胃口越来越大，超出自己的底限。因此，让步需要掌握恰当的时机。但是能够掌握合适时机做出让步是非常难的，需要凭借谈判者的经验和直觉来判断的。

• 让步的内容：在实际谈判中，双方可让步的内容是多样化的。

买方可以让步的内容一般有：批量订货（batch ordering），推迟交货期（delay delivery date），降低包装（reduce the requirements for sanitation），长期经销（long-term engagement）。

卖方可让步的内容一般有：降低某些项目的价格（lower the price of some items），为买方提供仓储和运输（provide the buyers with storage and delivery），提供方便的付款方式（provide convenient way of payment），培训技术人员（provide training for technicians）。

• 让步的方式：八种常用的让步方式分别为：冒险型、刺激型、希望型、妥协型、危险型、诱发型、虚伪型和愚蠢型。

2. 让步的原则。

• 让步的理由要清晰。让对方明确了解促成了己方的让步的原因，感觉到己方的诚意。例如：

> Based on an expanding market, we respond to your counter-offer by reducing the price by $300 per piece.
>
> We hope this concession can bring us more business, and we can establish a long-term relationship in the future.

• 让步的幅度和频率要适度。一次让步不能太大，否则会让对方认为自己的价格水分很大；让步不能太快，即使能做的让步，也要表现得非常勉强，要让对方意识到自己每次的让步都是艰难做出的，对方应该好好珍惜，共同推动谈判的进行。

例如：

This concession is our baseline. We have kept the price close to the cost of production.

10% discount is beyond my power. I have to consult the general manager first, then I will give you a definite answer.

• 让步要审慎。商务谈判中不要做无谓的让步。让步不能随意进行，每次的让步都要取得足够的回报。例如：

The price of X is acceptable, provided you increase the quantity of your order to...

3. 让步的策略。

• 于己无损策略：在谈判中，对方要求己方对某一项目做出让步，对方的要求有一定的合理性，但己方由于种种原因不能做出实质让步时，可采用于己无损的策略。

使用这一策略时，一定要有耐心倾听对方的表达，真诚地面对对方，坦诚地说明原因，以赢得对方的理解。例如：

Your requirements are reasonable, but now our scale of production is limited and we hope you can understand our case. Accordingly, we can assure that our price is the lowest one.

• 双赢策略：谈判时采用横向法则，即双方在各个议题上进行利益交换，而不是执着于某一议题，更有利于达成互惠互利式让步。例如：

How about meeting each other halfway? You bear charges of packing, and our price goes down 2% to meet your requirements.

• 刺激对方策略：在谈判中，如果己方的还价已经表示了很大的诚意，在某些项目上也做了让步，但对方对己方的让步没有太大的回应，这可能是由于对方认为己方对此次谈判更为重视。这时如果己方再次忍让，做出妥协更加不会得到对方的配合，所以适时地刺激对方是有必要的。例如：

A new product should be modestly priced, but your price does not come in line with the prevailing market. It is unwise of you to insist on that.

You have seen our sincerity, but if you insist on your price and refuse to make any concession, there will be not much point in further discussion.

4. 让步的实施。

• 让步前的准备。

让步利益的确定：让步不是“杀敌三百自损一千”的莽夫行为，它是围绕着会获得最大的目标利益而实施。所以在让步之前，先要明确此次谈判最终目的是什么，谈判对于双方的重要程度以及自己可接受的底线。

让步内容的选择：让步之前，要对谈判的各项内容进行具体分析，确定哪些项目可以适度让步，哪些是不能退缩必须坚持，并根据自己的让步内容判断对方可能给予的让步。

利益对象的选择：无论哪一方的让步都可以给对方带来一定的利益。但是获益者不只局限于对方公司，也可能是某个个人或某个小群体。不同的获益者会对己方的让步做出不同的回应。最佳的利益对象是对己方的让步最容易给予积极反应或回报的一方。

• 让步的具体实施。

寻找恰当的让步时机：根据谈判的实际情况，结合对对方心理的揣测，最佳让步时机应该是己方一做出让步，对方马上接受，没有犹豫的余地的时候。

确定合适的让步方式：之前提到八种常用的让步方式，在实际的谈判中，每种谈判方式并不是单独存在。根据不同的谈判情况要搭配利用多种让步方式，为最终的目标利益服务。

四、商务谈判的终结阶段

经过双方细致、耐心地磋商，谈判进入最后的终结阶段。谈判终结的方式一般是成交、中止和破裂三种。当双方利益有巨大冲突时，谈判不得不中止甚至宣布破裂。但对于一场有诚意的、双方都重视的、花费了一定时间和精力的谈判，我们希望是达成交易，谈判成功。本节主要讨论的是终结阶段的方式之一——成交。

（一）成交

1. 关于成交的一些概念。

• 成交的内涵：双方在谈判的具体内容方面达成了一致的观点。

• 成交的条件：磋商的结果在双方的接受范围之内，对双方都能带来一定的利益。

• 成交的时机：双方在“某个瞬间”心理契合，观点一致。这“某个瞬间”就是最佳的成交时机。

• 成交的信号：在即将成交时，谈判人员会有意无意地释放一些信号，如言语上多用肯定、积极、配合的回答；肢体行为放松、坐姿改变；面部表情轻松、自然。双方对成交信号的捕捉要准确，否则会毫无意义地延长谈判过程，甚至错失成交良机。

2. 谈判成交策略。

• 直取策略：谈判人员简明扼要地向对方提出成交的条件，直接要求成交。这种策略适合谈判双方比较熟悉或对方也有成交的打算但还在犹豫的情况。例如：

> We have accepted your requirements, so now shall we talk about your order quantity?
>
> This is not our first cooperation, and we have always been in good faith. So can you make a prompt delivery?

• 提供选择的引导策略：谈判一方向对方就某些问题提供两种或以上的解决方案，引导对方在已有的方案中进行选择。这样己方更容易掌握主动权，对方无论做出哪种选择己方都可以提前准备应对措施。例如：

> Which model will you order, the latest one or the classic one?
>
> Which terms of payment do you prefer, D/P or D/A?

这种引导策略可以减轻对方决策的心理负担，在良好的气氛中成交；同时也可以使谈判人员发挥顾问的作用，帮助对方顺利完成购买任务，因而具有广泛的用途。但是如果运用不当，可能会分散对方注意力，妨碍他们选择。运用此方法时应自然得体，既要主动热情，又不能操之过急，不能让对方有受人支配的感觉。

• 比较结果策略：在磋商阶段之后，如果一方仍犹豫不定，稍占主动的这方可以为对方分别分析成交的结果或中止的结果。

通过强调成交的好处来促使对方下定决心签约。进行不同的结果比较时态度要诚恳，分析要周密，让对方感觉站在他们的角度考虑问题。但是这种策略可能会增加对方的心理负担。例如：

> If we can make a deal this time, you will get sufficient fund which can enable you to enlarge your production scale, improve your working condition and develop new products. We believe it is hard for you to find out other buyer who can offer more favorable price than us. In that case, without enough investment the development of new models will be affected and your present leading status in this field will be changed.

3. 签订谈判备忘录。

• 回顾总结之前的谈判。应回顾的内容如下：已经解决了什么问题（The issues we have settled are...），哪些问题有待解决（There are some ones for further discussion, such as...)，达成的交易条件是否理想，己方进行了几次让步(We have made X times of concession.)，针对己方的让步对方的每次反应如何（For our first concession, your response is...)。

进行最后回顾的时间和形式没有固定要求。在回顾总结之后，双方要明确最终的报价和最后的让步。

• 确定采取何种策略完成交易。

• 起草谈判备忘录（Memo)：谈判备忘录就是谈判中的工作记录，它记载了双方各自的意见、交易条件以及对彼此的承诺，在签署正式协议时可作为参考。

谈判备忘录包括一些固定的结构：标题（title）或直接写“备忘录”（memo)，谈判双方情况（details of the two parties)，事项（specific terms)，双方签名（signature of two parties)。

备忘录不具备合同约束力。一经双方签字，谈判基本完成。

（二）签约

成交的体现方式就是双方最终签署谈判协议，合同生效。

谈判协议或合同不同于备忘录，它具有法律约束力，明确规定了双方的权利和义务。双方在享受各自权利的同时必须履行合同中规定的义务。

1. 起草合同时的注意事项。

起草合同的原则就是简明、流畅，条理清晰。

合同文书所使用的语言不能晦涩难懂，应该直接、简明扼要。尽量使用主动语态，避免被动语态。主动语态的句子更简短，措辞更精练，更能把意思表达明白。

在整个合同中，一方只能使用一个别称或简称。

2. 合同的整体结构。

包括开头部分即约首（initial part，preface of a treaty），正文部分即条款（body part，terms），结尾部分即约尾（ending part，end of a treaty）。

第三章　合同读译

一、项目合同简介

（一）概念

项目合同是指平等主体的自然人、法人、其他组织之间设立、变更、终止民事权利义务关系的协议。通俗的说法：当事人就某项事项权利义务自愿达成的协议。

（二）基本类型

1. 按照学理分类的项目合同。

• 有名合同与无名合同（以法律是否设有规范并赋予一个特定名称为标准）；

• 双务合同与单务合同（以给付义务是否由双方当事人互付为标准）；

• 有偿合同与无偿合同（以当事人取得权益是否须付相应代价为标准）；

• 诺成性合同与实践性合同（以合同的成立是否须付标的物或完成其他给付为标准）；

• 要式合同与不要式合同（以法律对合同的形式是否有特定要求为标准）；

• 主合同与从合同（以合同相互间的主从关系为标准）。

2. 按照合同法规定的有名合同的细分类型。

• 买卖合同（出卖人转移标的物的所有权于买受人，买受人支付价款的合同）；

• 赠与合同（赠与人将自己的财产无偿给予受赠人，受赠人表示接受与赠与的合同）；

• 借款合同（借款人向贷款人借款，到期返还借款并支付利息的合同）；

• 租赁合同（出租人将租赁物交付承租人使用、收益，承租人支付租金的合同）；

• 融资租赁合同（出租人根据承租人对出卖人、租赁物的选择，向出卖人购买租赁物，提供给承租人使用，承租人支付租金的合同）；

• 承揽合同（承揽人按照定做人的要求完成工作，交付工作成果，定做人给付报酬的合同）；

• 建筑施工合同（承包人进行工程建设，发包人支付价款的合同）；

• 运输合同（承运人将旅客或者货物从起运地点运输到约定地点，旅客、托运人或者收货人支付票款或者运输费的合同）；

• 技术合同（当事人就技术开发、转让、咨询或者服务订立的确立相互之间权利和义务的合同）；

• 保管合同（保管人保管寄存人交付的保管物，并返还该物的合同；仓储合同，指保管人储存存货人交付的仓储物，存货人支付仓储费的合同）；

• 委托合同（委托人和受托人约定，由受托人处理委托人事务的合同）；

• 行纪合同（行纪人以自己的名义为委托人从事贸易活动，委托人支付报酬的合同）；

• 居间合同（居间人向委托人报告订立合同的机会或者提供订立合同的媒介服务，委托人支付报酬的合同）；

• 供用电、水、气、热力合同（供给方向原使用方提供产品，使用方支付费用的合同）。

3. 根据实质内容分类的项目合同。

• 劳动人事合同，包括：劳动合同（labor contract）、保密协议（confidentiality agreement）、竞业禁止协议（non-compete agreement）、人事代理协议（human agency agreement）；

• 不动产合同，包括：商品房买卖合同（contact of sale of commodity houses）、租赁协议（tenancy agreement）、土地使用权出让、出租、转让合同（contract for assignment, lease and transfer of the right to the use of land）、抵押合同（mortgage contract）、贷款合同（loan contract）、物业管理合同（property management contract）、建设工程承包、安装合同（contract for construction engineering and installation of project）；

• 服务类合同，包括：技术服务合同（technical service agreement）、咨询合同（consultant agreement）、开发合同（development agreement）、转让合同（transfer agreement）、许可协议（licensing agreement）、代理协议（agency agreement）、保险合同（insurance contract）、融资协议（financing agreement）、风险投资管理协议（venture capital management agreement）、法律顾问协议（contract for legal consultant）；

• 公司类合同，包括：合资企业（joint venture contract）、章程（articles of association, corporate bylaw）、合伙协议（partnership agreement）、股权转让协议（agreement on assignment of equity interests）、和解协议（composition agreement)；

• 物流类合同，包括：买卖合同（sales contact）、采购合同（purchase contact）、运输合同（carriage contact）、进出口合同（import and export contact）、仓储保管合同（warehousing and safe-keeping contact）、补偿贸易合同（contact for compensation）；

• 人身类合同，包括：遗赠抚养协议（legacy-support agreement）、离婚协议（divorce agreement）。

（三）基本语言特色

项目合同是法律性的正式书面文件，语言正式，选词造句都极其考究。

1. 合同选词特色。

• 选词专业（professional）："may" "shall" "must" "may not" "shall not" 的使用在合同中要极为谨慎。权利义务的约定部分构成了合同的主体。这些词如选用不当，可能会引起纠纷。

"may" 旨在约定当事人的权利（可以做什么），"shall" 约定当事人的义务（应当做什么时候），"must" 用于强制性义务（必须做什么），"may not" 或 "shall not" 用于禁止性义务（不得做什么）。"may do" 不能说成 "can do" "shall do" 不能说成 "should do" 或 "ought to do"，"may not do" 在美国一些法律文件可以用 "shall not do"，但绝不能用 "can not do" 或 "must not do"。例如：

The parties hereto shall, first of all, settle any dispute arising from or in connection with the contract by friendly negotiations.

Should such negotiations fail, such dispute may be referred to the People's Court having jurisdiction on such dispute for settlement in the absence of any arbitration clause in the disputed contract or in default of agreement reached after such dispute occurs.

本句中的"shall"和"may"表达准确。出现争议后应当先行协商，所以采用了义务性"约定"，如果协商解决不了，作为当事人的权利，用选择性约定"may"也很妥当。上例的意思是"双方首先应通过友好协商，解决因合同而发生的或与合同有关的争议。如果协商未果，合同中又无仲裁条款约定或争议发生后未就仲裁达成一致的，可将争议提交有管辖权的人民法院解决。"

• 用语正式（formal）：合同英语有着严肃的风格，与其他英语作品有很大不同。

例如：

"因为"的短语多用"by virtue of"，远远多于"due to"一般不用"because of "；

"财务年度末"一般用"at the close of the fiscal year"，而不用"in the end of the fiscal year"；

"在……之前"一般用"prior to"，而不用"before"；

"关于"常用"as regards" "concerning"或"relating to"，而不会用"about"；

"事实上"用"in effect"，而不用"in fact"；

"开始"用"commencement"，而不用"start"或

"begin";

"停止做"用"cease to do",而不用"stop to do";

"何时开会并由某某主持"的表述为"The meeting shall be convened and presided by sb.",其中"召开"不用"hold"或"call",而用"convene","主持"不用"chair"或"be in charge of ",而用"preside";

"其他事项"用"miscellaneous",而不用"other matters/events";

"理解合同"用"construe a contract"或"comprehend a contract",而不用"understand a contract";

"认为"用"deem",用"consider"少,不用"think"或"believe";

"愿意做"用"intend to do"或"desire to do",而不用"want to do","wish to do"。

• 术语行话(technical):合同用词不以大众是否理解和接受为转移,它是合同语言准确表达的保障。

合同出现的"瑕疵"、"救济"、"不可抗力"、"管辖"、"损毁"、"灭失"等在英语中的表达分别为"defect" "remedy" "force majeure / Act of God" "jurisdiction" "damage and/or loss"。

另外,几乎每个合同都少不了"hereinafter referred to as" "whereas" "in witness whereof" "for and on behalf of" "hereby" "thereof"等虚词。这也是合同英语的特色。

2. 合同语句特色。

• 力求严谨,明白无误。

This Contract can only be altered, amended or

supplemented in accordance with documents signed and sealed by authorized representatives of both parties.

本合同只能按照双方授权代表签名盖章的文件进行修改或增补。

All activities of ABC Co. shall be governed by the laws, decrees and pertinent rules and regulations of China.

ABC公司的一切活动必须受中国的法律、法令和有关规章条例的管辖。

• 多用主动语态，少用被动语态。

Party B is hereby appointed by Party A as its exclusive sales agent in Singapore.

乙方被甲方委托为在新加坡的独家销售代理商。

上例中采用的是被动语态表达法，而在正式项目合同中更多采用的是主动语态表达法，例如：

Party A hereby appoints Party B as its exclusive sales agent in Singapore.

甲方委托乙方为在新加坡的独家销售代理商。

• 多用现在时，少用将来时。

尽管很多条款规定的是合同签订以后的事项，项目合同中一般采用现在时。例如：

Licensee may terminate this Contract 90 days after a written notice thereof is sent to Licensor upon the happening of one of the following events:

当有下列事件之一发生，被许可人提前 90 天向许可人发送书面通知后，可以终止合同：

Licensor becomes insolvent or a liquidator of Licensor is appointed.

许可人无力偿付债务或其破产清算人已被指定。

• 多用直接表达，少用间接表达。

This Article does not apply to bondholders who have not been paid in full.

本条款不适用于尚未全部偿付的债券持有者。

上例中这类间接表述用得少，而常用直接表达方式。例如：

This Article applies only to bondholders who have been paid in full.

本条款只适用于已全部偿付的债券持有者。

• 尽量使用一个动词，避免使用“动词＋名词＋介词”的同意短语

Party A shall make an appointment of its representative within 30 days after signing the Contract.

甲方应于签约后 30 天内指派其授权代表。

上例中宜用“appoint”代替“make an appointment of”。

Party A will give consideration to Party B's proposal of exclusive agency.

甲方愿意考虑乙方独家代理的建议。

上例中宜用“consider”代替“give consideration to”。

一份完整的项目合同通常可以分为标题（title）、前言（preamble）、正文（habendum）和证明（attestation）四大部分。起始部分的标题明确阐明合约的性质。前言是用最简单的说明，大略介绍合约订立的背景。正文部分的条款里包括依各种合约性质的不同而约定的特殊条款，以及不论何种类型合约都会出现的一般条款。最后的结尾证明部分则是当事人签名前的一段文字，是整份合约的结束。

二、项目合同的起始部分

合同的标题是为了使合同内容一目了然，合同标题本身没有特别的法律效力，且对合同内容也没有影响。如果合同书有封面的话，封面与合同的标题要保持一致。

（一）封面和目录

合同的封面和目录是合同最先映入我们眼帘的文字，但并非所有合同都有这两部分。一般来说，销售、购货确认书、订单、报价单、国际贸易流程中的商业单据，通常就没有封面和目录。只有正式合同、协议以及大型合同才会涉及封面和目录，这样才显得正式和慎重。

一般来说，合同封面并没有严格的式样，不过实践中形成了一些习惯性的做法。下面举例说明合同封面中的翻译要点。例如：

CONTRACT OF CIVIL WORKS
OF
LOAERDER－MUKARUS STRATEGIC HIGHWAY
BETWEEN
ORIENT ROAD AND BRIDGE ENGINEERING CORPORATION
AND
HIGHWAY AUTHORITY OF YEMENI REPUBLIC
MAY 28，2014

这是一页国际土木工程承包合同的封面，前面三行是合同的标题，下面有合同当事人的名称，末端是日期。英文合同封面讲究居中对称排列，全部使用大写加黑字母以示严谨。如果遇到介词，一般将介词单独成行，其他名词或词组按照意群排成多行。

翻译时，中文习惯于将合同双方当事人写在合同封面第一行，即：东方公路桥梁工程公司与也门公路局。

“CIVIL WORKS”这个术语本意是“土木工程”。整个文本就是一个土木工程建设合同，而“建设”更符合中国技术人员的习惯。

“CORPORATION”一般可以翻译成“总公司”，用以区分另一个英文单词“COMPANY”。其他表示公司的词语还有FIRM，BUSINESS，PARTNERS等，但这几个词语的规模都比“总公司”更小。

“AUTHORITY”翻译成“公路局”或“公路建设局”，不是“权威”。表示“局”的英文单词还有“BUREAU”“ADMINISTRATION”“DEPARTMENT”等。这些词语都应该遵循汉语和英文的表达习惯来翻译，具体问题具体分析。

原合同中的“between... and...”，可以按照中文习惯加上“与……沟通建设”的措辞。

中文的语序和英文很多时候是不同甚至是相反的，即中文要求定语在前，而被定语修饰的中心词在后面，所以，“合同”二字应该最后译出。上例翻译参考如下：

东方公路桥梁工程总公司与也门共和国公路局 共同建设洛德尔—木卡拉斯战略公路 合同 2014 年 5 月 28 日

在正式合同、协议和大型合同中，目录（Table of Contents）页紧跟在封面页之后。目录的英文字母一般都是大写字母。目录的内容就是合同文本的提纲，但目录通常只包含合同的一级标题，最多只列出二级标题，更次级的内容标题只出现在合同正文里。例如：

CONTENTS

这是一个国际补偿贸易合同的目录，从篇幅看，大约有三十页，属于一个中等规模的正式合同。合同中第八条到第十四条是任何合同中常见的一般条款。

“PREAMBLE”翻译成“前言”、“导言”或者“当事人”，但是通常不宜译成“序言”，因为这个词在中文里常指著作类书籍的开头语。

第一条中“TRANSACTIONS”指的是本项补偿贸易合同的具体内容，实际上是该合同的标的，因此不能简单翻译成“交易”或“贸易”，而应该根据合同内容表述为“贸易内容”

或“贸易事宜”。

第十条“WARRANTY”不能直接翻译成“担保”或“保证”。这样在目录中显得不明确。此条款最好翻译成“履约担保”或“履约保证”，这与签订合同后常见的“履约保函”和“履约保证金”相呼应。

第十一条“AMENDMENT”原意是“修订”，但在合同语言里习惯表达为“变更”。根据合同内容，这个条款最好翻译为“合同条款的变更”。上例参考译文如下：

目录

三、项目合同的引入部分

(一) 第一节

项目合同在标题之后，各式各样的条款出现之前，通常会先有一段很简略地介绍合约规范内容之人、事、时、地、物等背景，让阅读合约的人在接触冗长复杂的主文前，先有一个基础的认识与心理准备。

通常来讲，引入部分分为两个小节：第一小节文字叫作“commencement”，也就是合约的开场白，内容在说明合约当事人姓名或名称、当事人的国籍与住所或主营业所、订约日期等等。例如：

This Share Purchase Agreement is made on the 3rd day of May, 1991 by and between: (1) ENTERPRISES HOJAEC SA, a company organized and existing under the laws of France and having its registered office at 89 rue Albert Thomas, 75010 Paris and (2) Mark Gilbert Handerson, an individual with nationality of the United States of America (Passport No. 12345678), residing at 2199 Palm Street, Pleasant Hill, California 94509, USA.

本股份收购契约订立于公元一九九一年五月三

日，双方当事人为：（1）依法国法律组织设立的 ENTERPRISES HOJAEC SA 公司，注册所在地为 48 rue Albert Thomas，75010 Paris，与（2）美国籍的马克·吉尔伯特·汉德森（护照号码 12345678），居住于美国加利福尼亚普莱森特希尔棕榈街 2199 号（94509）。

再如：

This Contract is made and entered into through friendly negotiation by and between China ________ Corporation, a corporation organized and existing under the laws of the People's Republic of China (hereinafter referred to as "the Buyer"), as one party and __________, a corporation organized and existing under the laws of __________ (hereinafter referred to as "the Seller"), as the other party, under the following terms and conditions.

中国某公司（根据中华人民共和国法律成立注册的公司，以下简称甲方）为一方，与某公司（根据某国法律成立注册的公司，以下简称乙方）为另一方，双方通过友好协商同意就下列条款签订本合同。

（二）第二节

合同引入部分的第二节是说明条款"鉴于"（whereas）、"叙述"（recital）或"背景"（background）部分。在现代英文合同中，有时也将说明条款放在合同正文中。一般来说合同中有无说明条款，不会影响其法律效力。但要注意以下两点：第一，合同正文不够明确时，说明条款的内容就被视为明确合同内容，把握当事人真正意图的重要资料。第二，在说明条款中写入事实的当事人，不能主张与此相反的阐述。因此制作说明条款也不能草率，应在深思熟虑后书写。该小节通常包括以下内容：

1. 合同双（各）方的背景情况介绍。

AMD engages through its Communication Products Division (CPD) in the design, development, manufacture and sale of telecommunication products for public communications infrastructure systems, customer premise equipment and cordless telephony applications.

AMD公司是通过其通讯产品部门进行公共通讯产品的设计、研发、制造的企业，并销售公共通讯系统、客户预订设备和无线通讯产品。

2. 合同目的。

WHEREAS PARTY A and PARTY B have agreed to establish a joint venture according to terms and conditions of this joint venture contract to jointly develop the [PROJECT].

鉴于甲方和乙方同意按照本合营合同的条件和条款设立合资企业，共同开发×项目。

3. 合同的背景情况。

Whereas Party C intends to buy the whole shares of × held by Party A, adhering to the principals of equality and mutual benefit, the parties have reached the following agreement (the "Agreement") after friendly consultations regarding the share transfer matters.

鉴于丙方拟受让甲方在×公司的全部股权，现合同各方经友好协商，本着平等互利的原则，应上述股权转让事宜达成如下条款。

Whereas, Manufacturer is engaged in the manufacture and sale of the Products;

Whereas, Manufacturer is desirous of selling the Products in the Territory;

Whereas, Distributor is engaged in the importation and distribution of the related products of the Products in the Territory; and

Whereas, Distributor is desirous of becoming a distributor of the Products in the Territory.

Now Therefore, the parties hereto agree as follows:

(note: "Manufacturer", "Products", "Territory", and "Distributor" are all to be defined in other parts of the contract.)

制造人乃从事本商品制造之公司。

制造人希望在经销区域进行本商品之销售。

销售人乃在经销区域从事与本商品相关商品进口与销售之公司。

销售人希望能在经销区域代销本商品。

基于以上之认识，双方当事人遂就下列各事项达成协议：

（提示：文中提到的制造人、本商品、经销区域及经销商都应该在合约的其他部分加以定义。）

WHEREAS, this Agreement is supplemental to an agreement dated 5 December 1989 between the parties to this Agreement (“the Principal Agreement”) under which the Purchaser agreed to buy certain assets of the Vendor for an aggregate sum of £3 million.

本合约是为补充双方当事人前于公元一九八九年十二月五日业已缔结之合约（以下称主合约）所订立，买方于主合约中同意向卖方购买总价值三百万英镑的资产。

四、项目合同的正文部分

项目合同正文（habendum）主要是条款部分。此部分包含的条款千差万别，合同的一般性条款（general conditions），也称作通用条款，是任何一份合同得以成立的法律基础。一般性条款的作用是对整个合同内容从法律意义上进行定性说明，确定合同订立人、标的物以及主要合同术语的法律地位。

一般性条款通常涉及各类合同的基本或共有内容，包括：定义条款、合同效力条款、担保条款、保密性条款、转让与变更条款、赔偿条款、不可抗力条款、违约条款、仲裁条款、期限与终止条款、管辖法律条款、语言条款和通知条款。以下就上述部分条款予以读译解析。

（一）定义条款（definitions）

合同中的重要概念可用定义条款加以定义。这样做的优点是避免合同在用语上的烦琐；避免合同内容在理论上缺少一贯性。在定义条款中被下了定义的词语，在以后的各项条款中出现时必须用大写字母表示。例如：

> "Business Day" means, in respect of Party A and any action to be taken by Party B in the PRC, any day on which the companies in the PRC are generally open for business in the PRC, including a Saturday or Sunday which the PRC government temporarily declares to be a working day ("Working Rest Day"), but excluding a statutory holiday, or a Saturday or Sunday other than a Working Rest Day; in respect of any action to be taken by Party B in [Party B Home Country], any day on which the companies in [Party B Home Country] are generally open for business in [Party B Home Country].
>
> "工作日"就甲方而言，指中华人民共和国境内公司通常对外营业的任何一日，包括中国政府宣

布为临时工作日的星期六或星期日（“调休工作日”），但不包括法定节假日以及调休工作日以外的星期六或星期日；就乙方而言，指乙方所在国境内公司通常对外营业的任何一日。

再如：

“Address” means — (a) in relation to an individual, his usual residential or business address; and (b) in relation to a corporation, its registered or principal office in the People's Republic of China.

“地址”就自然人而言，指通常之居所或工作场所；就公司而言，指位于中华人民共和国之注册所在地或主营业所。

定义条款一般会由一个开头句进行概括，如“本合同中的下列词语含义如下”。概括起来，定义条款中常用的句型和用词包括“shall refer to”“means”“shall mean”和“shall have the meaning of”四种，偶尔用“shall be construed as”。定义条款一般出现在大型合同中，并且定义内容只针对合同、协议本身，因而开头处需明确说明，固定用“For the purpose of this Agreement”，可以译成“仅限于本协议中”。“term”是一词多义的单词，译成汉语有“词语”“术语”“条款”等意思，在定义条款中，多指“词语”而不应译为“条款”。一些定义条款中的词语往往已经有固定的汉语表达，如“business day”一般均译为“营业日”，“PRC”一般指中华人民共和国。但有时这些词语也不一定总是这样的含义，因此要具体问题具体分析。“including but not limited to”为固定表达，译为“包括但不限于”。这类表达不应随意翻译，应该遵循惯例。合同语言的特点是严谨、简洁，不能用一些口语式的表达。本合同中indicated 就不应简单翻译成“暗示”、“显示”。在翻译一些合同法律术语时，要注意不能根据辞典上的释义简单套用，而一定要依照法律或行业固有的习惯用语来翻译。如本合同中的“贷款协定”“担保文件”“资产转让协定”“转让通告”等。例如：

For the purpose of this Agreement, unless the context otherwise requires, the following terms shall have the meanings indicated below:

a. “Asset Document” means all the documents sets out in Schedule I, including but not limited to, the loan agreements, security documents, assets transfer agreements, transfer notices, settlement agreements (if any), court judgments and/or orders in relation to the loans under such loan agreements, and any other relevant documents, agreements or instruments.

b. “Business Day” means any day other than a Saturday, Sunday or day that is a legal holiday in the PRC or, if any payments to be made hereunder are denominated in U. S. dollars, a legal holiday in New York, U. S. A.

c. “PRC” means the People's Republic of China. For the purpose of this Agreement, PRC does not include Hong Kong, Macau and Taiwan.

本合同中的下列词语，除文意另有所指外，含义如下：

(1) "资产文件"指所有在表1中列出的文件，包括但并不限于贷款协议、安全文档、资产转移协议、转移声明、结算协议（如存在）、法院判决与/或此贷款协定下与贷款相关的法院规定以及其他相关文件、协定和文书。

(2) "营业日"指除周六、周日、中华人民共和国的法定假日及美国纽约的法定假日——如以美元支付的话——以外的任一日。

(3) PRC 指中华人民共和国。在本协议中，PRC 不包括香港、澳门和台湾地区。

(二) 担保条款 (warranty)

担保条款指项目合同中的当事人一方或双方针对过去曾经发生或现在存在、可能影响合约效力的一些事实，保证确实不虚假的条款。在几乎所有合同中都存在担保条款，目的是确实保障双方权益。在国际贸易的担保条款中，经常会出现比较明显的表示保证的词汇，虽然在语言学上可以将"Representation""Warranty"和"Covenant"区别开来，但是在英文合约的实际撰写上，常常把它们放在同一个条款里，统称为"Representations and Warrants"或是"Covenants and Warrants"。由此可见，法律英语好用重复词语的特征。例如：

The Contractor represents and warrants that the "Contractor" is empowered legally, and this Contract has been duly authorized, executed and delivered by the "Contractor", and constitutes a legal, valid and binding obligation of the "Contractor", enforceable in accordance with its terms.

承包商声明并保证，承包商经依法授权，本合同经承包商授权、签署并提交对方，对承包商形成合法、有效、具有法律约束力的合同责任，依照本合同规定具有强制执行效力。

上例中的第一个动词"represents"通常理解为"代表"，但在法律英语中，适合翻译成"声明"。动词"empowered"表示某人被授予权力，而汉语不习惯被动语态，所以翻译成"经授权"为好。动词"executed"在此不是"执行"的意思，从语境来看，应该是"签字"之意。为了正式起见，最好译为"签署"。动词"delivered"的基本含义类似于"give"，但为了显得正式可以译为"提交"或"提供"。最后的短语"enforceable in accordance with its terms"，在文中充当"obligation"的定语，如果直接翻译为定语，句子就会太长且表达意思不清楚，所以采用拆开句子成分的策略，另起一句，翻译成"依照本合同规定具有强制执行效力"。

（三）期限条款（term）

期限条款指合同效力的生效期及终止期，这是合同中必须明确表示的内容。合同到期就会自动失效，如需更新时，一定要明确记载更新手续及延长期间。例如：

Period of Agreement (Duration) This Agreement comes into force on the date on which it approved by the Chinese Government and continues for five years. On the expiry of the period A may continue this Agreement for further five years by twelve months' prior written notice to B.

合同期限：本合同从中国政府批准之日其生效，合同期限为 5 年。在合同期限届满前 12 个月，A 方可向 B 方发出书面通知，将本合同再续期 5 年。

(四) 通知条款 (notify)

通知条款是对合同双（各）方在履行合同过程中相互送达信息的方式以及视为送达的条件进行约定。一般来讲，要写明合同双（双）方的通信地址、传真号、联系电话、联络人以及送达成功的具体条件。例如：

This Agreement shall be valid and remain in force for a period of three (3) years commencing from the date appearing first above written upon the signing of both Party A and Party B and shall be extended for another period of three (3) years on the same terms and conditions unless either of the parties hereto gives the other party at least thirty (30) days prior written notice to terminate this Agreement prior to the expiration of the original term.

本合约须从上面首次写明的甲方和乙方签订本约的日期起生效并保持效力三年，并将按同样条件延长三年，否则与约任何一方至少须在原定时间期满前三十天给予另一方提前终止本合约的书面通知。

10—15 days prior to the date of shipment, the Buyer shall inform the Seller by cable or telex of the contract number, name of vessel, ETA of vessel, quantity to be loaded and the name of shipping agent, so as to enable the Seller to contact the shipping agent direct and arrange the shipment of the goods. The Seller shall advise by cable or telex in time the Buyer of the result thereof. Should, for certain reasons, it become necessary for the Buyer to replace the named vessel with another one, or should the named vessel arrive at the port of shipment earlier or later than the date of arrival as previously notified to the Seller, the Buyer or its shipping agent shall advise the Seller to this effect in due time. The Seller shall also keep in close contact with the agent or the Buyer.

货物装运日前10—15天，买方应以电报或电传通知卖方合同号、船只预计到港日期、装运数量及船运代理人的名称。以便卖方经与该船运代理人联系及安排货物的装运。卖方应将联系结果通过电报或电传及时报告买方。如买方因故需要变更船只或者船只比预先通知卖方的日期提前或推迟到达装运港口，买方或其船运代理人应及时通知卖方。卖方亦应与买方的运输代理或买方保持密切联系。

During the Term, each Party may change its particulars for receipt of notices at any time by notice given to the other Party in accordance with this Article 19.7.

在合同期限内，一方可随时根据第19.7条规定通知另一方变更通知送达地址。

（五）修订条款（modification）

修订条款为合同常用条款。主要规定了合同修订的方式与途径。例如：书面合同只能以书面方式进行修订，口头修订内容无效。例如：

Any modification, amendment or waiver of any of the provisions of this Agreement must otherwise be made in writing and duly signed by the parties hereto.

对本“协议”任何规定的任何变更、修改或免责必须另以书面形式做出，并经各方正式签字。

During the period of validity of the agreement, either party shall be entitled to make proposal of amendment to the agreement and the agreement amended shall go into effect with the signature of the two parties.

在协议的有效期内，任何一方都有权提出对协议进行修改，修改后的协议经过双方签署后才能够生效。

（六）不可抗力条款（force majeure）

不可抗力条款是一种免责条款，即免除由于不可抗力事件而违约的一方的违约责任。一般应规定的内容包括：不可抗力事件的定义（definition of force majeure）以及不可抗力事件的后果（consequences of force majeure）。在不可抗力条款中，两者属于因果关系，难以截然分开。例如：

Neither party of this Agreement, directly or indirectly owing to any causes or circumstances beyond its control, including Acts of God, Governmental orders or restriction, war, warlike conditions, revolutions, strike, lockout, fire and flood.

本合同任何一方当事人对直接或间接地由于其无法控制的原因或情况包括自然灾害、政府命令或限制、战争、类战争状态、革命、罢工、工厂被关闭、火灾、水灾等而未能履行或延迟履行合同或合同一部分的行为，不负任何责任。

If because of any event of Force Majeure, including without limitation, explosion, fire, lighting stride, earthquake, hurricane, war, riot, civil disturbance or strike, or the enactment, rescission of amendment of any law, regulation, rule, decree or practice of any Chinese governmental authority, a party is unable to continue to operate or otherwise perform its obligations hereunder for a period of more than thirty days, then the other party may terminate this Agreement by thirty days prior written notice to the first party, provided that the cause for termination has not been remedied within the thirty days period of notice.

如因不可抗力的原因，包括但并不限于爆炸、火灾、地震、台风、战争、暴乱、内乱、罢工，或中国政府部门新近颁布、废除、修改的相关法律、规章、政令等，协议一方无法在三十天内继续履行合同条约，另一方可提前三十天以书面形式提出终止协议请求，若造成协议终止的原因未在通知的三十天内得以改善，本协议终止。

下例中不可抗力条款并没有用列举式叙述战争、地震、水灾、暴风雨、雪灾或其他不可抗力的具体情形，而是以综合式提示各方注意。在实施中，如若真的遭遇不可抗力，当事人一般还要提供由权威机构出示的证明文件。在语言上，本例是一个带有由"should"引导的倒装虚拟条件句的主从复合句。使用了一个含有虚拟语气的倒装条件句，可以翻译成"如果因为……"的条件句。名词化表达是英语合同的一个明显特点，如条款中的"occurrence"等词，在翻译过程中，可以根据汉语表达习惯的特点与需要转换成汉语的动词，如译成"发生"。"shall"是英文合同中常见词汇，经常表示"理应""应该"的意思，并且在英文中不可以用"be going to"或"will"来代替，在翻译成汉语时也要注意选词的准确性，突出语气上的强制性。分词在英文合同中也很常用，可能会做定语或状语。由于汉语中没有类似分词结构的表达习惯，因此在翻译时，可以将下例中的“stipulating”和“stating”等词翻译成动词。

Should any party be prevented from performing the terms and conditions of this Agreement due to the occurrence of any event of force majeure after the date hereof, the prevented party shall send notice to the other party within fourteen (14) Business Days from the occurrence of the event of force majeure stipulating the occurrence of the event of force majeure and stating in the notice that such event is an event of force majeure.

如因不可抗力原因，协议一方受阻无法履行本协议所约定条款，受阻方需再不可抗力事件发生后14天内通知对方，并明述不可抗力事件本身及其不可抗力性所在。

（七）保密条款（non-disclosure or No Publicity）

保密条款规定合同双（各）方对本合同内容以及在本合同协商、签订、履行过程中所得知的其他各方的信息要承担保密义务。例如：

The existence of this Contract, as well as its content, shall be held in confidence by both Parties and only disclosed as may be agreed to by both Parties or as may be required to meet securities disclosure or export permit requirements. Neither Party shall make public statements or issue publicity or media releases with regard to this Contract or the relationship between the Parties without the prior written approval of the other Party.

双方应对本合同的存在及其内容保密，只有在双方均同意的情况下（或者根据有关证券市场规定须披露或为获得出口许可证须披露的情况下）方可向有关方披露。未经对方事先书面同意，任何一方均不得就本合同或双方的关系发表公开声明或发布宣传或新闻稿。

From time to time prior to and during the term of this Contract either Party (“disclosing Party”) has disclosed or may disclose Confidential Information to the other Party (“Receiving Party”). The receiving Party shall, during the term of this Contract and for two years thereafter: (a) maintain the confidentiality of Confidential Information; (b) not to use Confidential Information for any purpose other than those specifically set out in this Contract; and (c) not disclose any such Confidential Information to any person or entity, except to its employees or employees of its Affiliates, its agents, attorneys, accountants and other advisors who need to know such information to perform their responsibilities and who have signed written confidentiality contracts containing terms at least as stringent as the terms provided in this Article.

本合同订立前以及在本合同期间，一方（“披露方”）曾经或者可能不时向对方（“受方”）披露该方的保密资料。在本合同期限内以及随后2年间，受方必须：对保密资料进行保密；不为除合同明确规定的目的之外的其他目的使用保密资料；除为履行其职责而确有必要知悉保密资料的该方雇员（或其关联机构、该方律师、会计师或其他顾问的雇员）外，不向其他任何人披露，且上述人员须签署书面保密协议，其中保密义务的严格程序不得低于本条的规定。

（八）转让条款（assignment or successors and assignment）

转让条款指合同双（各）方可约定合同不可转让或者合同转让的程序，同时，还可以约定，如果合同转让，受让方有完全约束力。例如：

The renouncing client can be substituted by another person provided that:

明示放弃合同的当事方可以由其他人受让。只要受让人符合以下条件：

The Distributor may not assign in whole or in part any of its rights hereunder or any rights arising from any individual order for the purchase of the Products without the prior written consent of Supplier. The Supplier shall be entitled to assign in whole or in part any of its obligations hereunder or arising from any individual order for the purchase of the Products to any of its Affiliates or suppliers solely upon written notice to Distributor, provided that Supplier shall remain fully liable for the performance of such obligations.

未经供应商事先书面同意，经销商不得部分或全部转让本合同项下的权利，也不得转让由单个订单产生的任何权利。供应商以书面通知经销商，可将本合同项下的全部或部分义务或由单个订单产生的任何义务转让给其任何关联机构或供货商，但是供应商应该继续对其合同项下义务的履行负责。

（九）损害赔偿条款（indemnification）

损害赔偿条款是减少合同风险的一个重要条款。该条款主要约定在第三者对合同提出权利主张时，另一缔约方应当对此承担责任。通常情况下，另一缔约方必须支付全部的防御性诉讼费用，以及全部的支付给第三者的和解费用或者第三者胜诉后造成的所有损失。例如：

Party A agrees to indemnify and hold Party B harmless from any claim or demand, including reasonable attorneys' fees, made by any third party due to or arising out of Party A's use of the Site, the violation of this Agreement by Party A, or the infringement by Party A, or other user of the Site using Party A's login name and password, of any intellectual property or other right of any person or entity.

甲方同意对乙方因甲方使用网站或甲方违反本协议或因甲方或其他使用甲方之登记名称及密码而使用网站的使用者，侵犯任何知识产权或任何其他人士或单位的其他权利所造成的损失做出赔偿及保证乙方不招致任何索偿或索求，包括合理的律师费用。

Contractor agrees to protect, defend, indemnify and hold harmless company, its parent, subsidiaries and affiliated companies, and its and their employees, subcontractors and its and their insurers from and against any claim, demand, cause of action, loss, expense award, obligation to indemnify another, judgment or liability on account of illness, injury or death to the employees of contractor and contractor's subcontractors and/or damage to or loss or destruction of the property of contractor arising directly or indirectly out of the performance of this contract regardless of omissions or negligence, in whole or in any part, of company.

承包商同意保护、辩护、赔偿和保证公司、其上级公司、下属公司和关联公司及其雇员、次承包商和其保险公司不承担在履行本合同过程中，不论公司是否存在部分或全部的不作为或疏忽的责任，直接或间接所导致的承包商和次承包商的雇员生病、受伤或死亡以及承包商的财产所遭受的毁损灭失相关的任何诉求、要求、诉因、损失、费用、对他方的赔偿义务、判决或赔偿责任。

赔偿是对某种损失负有法律责任的一方（受偿方）将该损失转移给另一方（赔偿方）的权力。赔偿权通常因明确的合同承诺而生。近年来，随着中国成为出口大国，无论是面对欧美国家还是第三世界国家，我国对外贸易企业均感受到这种压力。因此，学习和研究翻译赔偿条款在签订合同时就是不可以忽视的一个重点内容。以下为一些常见的索赔条款词汇：

specification 规格
in conformity with... 与……相符
be liable for... 对……负法律责任
on the strength of 基于，根据
inspection certificate 检验证书
compensation 赔偿
quality guarantee period 质量保证期
lodge a claim against sb. 向……提出索赔
in case (of)... 在……情况下，如，假如
in any case 在任何情况下

In case the payment is not made through L/C, the sellers shall pay the penalty counted as above to the buyers as soon as possible.

在未采用信用证的情况下，卖方应将上述方法计算的违约金即付买方。

In case of breach of this contract by Employer, the employer agrees to pay the amount stated in Section 5 as mitigated damages, plus reasonable attorney's fees, court costs, and legal interest.

在雇主违反本合同情况下，雇主同意支付第五条款中提到的金额以赔偿损失，并需支付合理的律师费用、法庭费用及法定利息。

Said amount is non-returnable and remains definitely acquired by the Licensor in any case and whatever may be the destiny of this agreement.

以上支付的金额不退还，无论本协议发生什么情况，将由许可人拥有。

Within 30 days after the arrival of the goods at the destination, should the goods be found damaged, missing or the quality, specifications or quantity not in conformity with the stipulations of the contract except those claims for which the insurance company or the owners of the vessel are liable, the Buyers shall have the right on the strength of the inspection certificate issued by the C. C. I. C. and the relative documents to claim for compensation to the Sellers. In case the claim period above specified is not in conformity with the quality guarantee period, during the quality guarantee period, the Buyers shall have rights to lodge claims for compensation against the Sellers concerning the quality guarantee.

在货到目的港后30天内，如发现货物有损坏、丢失或质量、规格或数量与合同不符，除属保险公司或船方责任外，买方有权凭中国商检出具的检验证书或有关文件向卖方索赔。如上述规定之索赔期与质量保证期不一致，在质量保证期限内，买方有权就质量保证条款之内容向卖方提出索赔。

上例中条款的句子非常长，因此，为了准确理解并翻译其含义，我们首先应该分析理解其结构。这是个主从复合句，主句部分是“the Buyers shall have rights to lodge claims for compensation against the Sellers”（买方有权就质量保证条款之内容向卖方提出索赔）。“on the strength of the inspection certificate issued by the C. C. I. C. and the relative documents ”是句中的状语部分。主句前“should the goods be found damaged, missing or the quality, specifications or quantity not in conformity with the stipulations of the contract except those claims for which the insurance company or the owners of the vessel are liable”是条件状语从句，相当于“if the goods should be found damaged, missing, or...”。“should”是商务合同中使用频率很高的词，通常用于表示“假设”的条件句中。由于合同是非常正式的文体，因而合同中常常使用省略IF的虚拟条件句。根据其表达的含义，我们需要在翻译时将“if”译出。

再看一个例子：

Indemnitor ’s Right to Dispute Claim. An indemnitor has the right, by written notice, for a

30-day period, to dispute its liability to an Indemnitee with respect to a Claim. The 30-day period begins the day after the Indemnitor's receipt of the Indemnitee's notice pursuant to subsection (a) and ends at 5：00 p. m. on the 30th day.

赔偿方的赔偿异议权。赔偿方有权在三十天期限内以书面通知的方式究其因任何索赔而应对受偿方承担的责任提出异议。该三十天期限自赔偿方收悉受偿方依据次项（a）规定发出的通知之日起至第三十天下午五点止。

上例中第一个短语独立写成了句子，表示本条款的主旨。通常说的"索赔"和"理赔"发生在保险公司与投保人之间，而在本例中的索赔与赔偿发生在合同双方当事人之间，赔偿人应对对方的索赔态度及行为也不称为"理赔"，而是"赔偿异议（dispute)"。由于不是发生在保险公司的业务或其他一般民事纠纷，所以"right to dispute claim"可以翻译为"赔偿异议权"。"dispute its liability"可以翻译为"对……提出异议"。词组"with respect to"也是"关于"的意思，不过可以用更为严谨的词语"究其"。"pursuant to"是非常正式而严谨的一个短语，意为"根据"。"subsection (a)"可以译为"次项"。中文对法律条款的分级措辞一般分为章、节、条、款、项。

（十）争议解决条款（dispute resolution）

争议解决条款约定与合同有关的争议解决方式，可以选择诉讼，也可以选择仲裁。

The single or partial exercise of any right,

power or privilege hereunder by any party shall not preclude any other or further exercise thereof or of any other right, power or privilege hereunder.

任何一方单独或部分行使本协议下的任何权利、权力或特权不得妨碍以任何其他方式或进一步行使该等权利、权力或特权或本协议的任何其他权利、权力或特权。

In the event such dispute is not resolved through consultations within [sixty (60)] days after the date such consultations were first requested in writing by a Party, then any Party may submit the dispute for arbitration in [Beijing] before the China International Economic and Trade Arbitration Commission ("CIETAC") in accordance with CIETAC Arbitration Rules then in force, and as amended by this Article 18.2 ("Arbitration Rules").

如果某一争议未在一方首次书面提出进行磋商之日后［六十（60）］日内通过友好协商解决，则任何一方可将该争议提交中国国际经济贸易仲裁委员会（"贸仲会"）在［北京］按照当时有效的贸仲会仲裁程序规则，并由本第 18.2 条规定作为修订（"仲裁规则"）进行仲裁。

五、项目合同的结尾部分

（一）证明

证明（attestation）是项目合同最后一个部分，即证明部分与当事人的签名。所谓结尾辞指的是在当事人签名之前经常会出现一段文字，相当于中文合同中“双方签字盖章，特此为证”。除了表明签名人确实为正当授权的代表外，还会具明签名的日期。至于签名档的部分，如果当事人是公司的话，除了代表人的签名以外，还要加盖公司印鉴，并且通常会注明代表人的职务（title）。例如：

BOARD OF DIRECTORS' RESOLUTION DESIGNATING A PURCHASING AGENT

Pursuant to a duly made, seconded, and carried motion the Board of Directors of ________________ (hereinafter referred to as Corporation) adopted the following resolution by a unanimous vote:

RESOLVED, that ________________________ is hereby appointed Purchasing Agent of this Corporation with limited authority to make purchases in the Corporation's name and behalf. Under no circumstances will the Purchasing Agent have real or apparent authority to make a purchase for the Corporation if the dollar amount of said purchase or the total dollar amount of an installment purchase will exceed the amount of ________________ dollars ($ ____________) .

I The undersigned, ____________________, certifies that he or she is the duly appointed Secretary of ________________ Corporation and that the above is a true and correct copy of a resolution duly adopted at a meeting of the directors thereof, convened and held in accordance with law and the Bylaws of said Corporation on ______________, (Date) and that such resolution is now in full force and effect.

IN WITNESS THEREOF, I have affixed my name as Secretary of ________________ Corporation and have attached the seal of __________________ Corporation to this resolution.

Dated: ____________________________________

Secretary

Seal:

董事会决议：

任命采购员：

就已第二次提起到董事会的动议，本公司董事会全体一致通过如下决议：

兹决议，本公司授权______为本公司采购员，以本公司名义代表本公司对外采买。但其单笔采购金额或分期购买的总额不得超过______美元。超过该数额该采购员概无真实或表见代理权。

我，签字人，证明______，他/她是本公司正式任命的秘书，以上是本公司董事会决议的真实准确的副本，该决议系按法律和本公司章程在*年*月*日召开的董事会上正式通过，现完全有效。

作为公司秘书我签字并盖公司印鉴于该决议，特此为证。

日期：*年*月*日

秘书：（签字）

公司印鉴：（盖章）

再如：

BEFORE ME, a Notary Public in and for said County, personally appeared Timothy J. Gunter and Daniel L. Webb, known to me to be the person(s) who, as Secretary and Assistant Secretary, respectively, of INDUSTRIAL DEVELOPMENTS INTERNATIONAL, INC., the corporation which executed the foregoing instrument in its capacity as Landlord, signed the same, and acknowledged to me that they did so sign said instrument in the name and upon behalf of said corporation as officers of said corporation, that the same is their free act and deed as such officers, respectively, and they were duly authorized thereunto by its board of directors; and that the seal affixed to said instrument is the corporate seal of said corporation. IN TESTIMONY WHEREOF, I have hereunto subscribed my name, and affixed my official seal, this 15th day of March, 1999。

我是本县公证员，兹证明汤姆斯·刚特与丹尼尔·韦伯两人分别为国际产业发展有限公司的秘书和秘书助理。该公司制作并签署了以土地产权为内容的上述文件。签署人是上述公司的官员，以上述公司的名义并代表上述公司进行的签署。他们经公司合法授权，分别履行的他们的公司官员职务行为，并盖以公司法人印章。特此证明，证明人签字于1999年3月15日。

有些项目合同还包括附录（schedule, addendum, annex, exhibit, attachment, list, table）。附录部分作为对正文条款的补充，不是所有英文合同都有的一项。例如：

Appendices hereof shall be integral parts of Contract and have the same legal force as the text of Contract itself. The text of Contract shall prevail in case of any discrepancies between the text of Contract and Appendices.

本合同的附件为本合同不可分割的组成部分，与合同正文具有同等法律效力。如合同正文与附件有矛盾之处，合同正文内容优先。

再如：

THE SCHEDULE ABOVE REFERRED TO

1. To manage, maintain and promote the business of the Company

2. To attend personally during the usual hours of business and to supervise and control the business and to be accessible to customers and employees of the Company.

3. To keep the usual books of account.

4. To pay daily all money received in the business into the Company's bank account.

5. Generally to protect the interests of the Company.

上文提及的附录是指：

1. 管理，维持并促进公司的经营

2. 亲自参与公司的日常经营，监管经营，对本公司的客户和员工平易近人。

3. 保管日常账册。

4. 支付日常公司经营到账的款项

5. 广泛地保护公司的利益

（二）合同结尾

合同的结尾也称为合同最后条款，写在合同的结尾部分。结尾条款主要应明确的内容有合同使用的文字及其效力(languages in which the contract is to be written and its validity)。除了明确使用的文字及其效力外，有时还应订立对合同进行修改或补充的内容。下面提供一些常见的最后条款范例：

This contract is made out in two originals, each copy written in Chinese and English languages, both texts being equally valid. In case of any divergence of interpretation, the Chinese text shall prevail.

本合同正文一式两份，均以中文和英文书写，两种文本具有同等效力。若对其解释产生异议，则以中文文本为准。

Any amendment and/or supplement to this contract shall be valid only after the authorized representatives of both parties have signed written document(s), forming integral part(s) of this Contract.

本合同的任何修改和（或）补充，只有在双方授权的代表在书面文件上签字才能生效，并为本合同不可分割的组成部分。

This contract shall come into force after the signatures by the authorized representatives of both parties.

本合同将在双方授权的代表签字后正式生效。

This Agreement is written in Chinese and English languages and is signed in triplicate by Party A and Party B as follows:

本合同用中英文两种语言书写，一式三份，经甲乙双方签字如下：

In case of difference of interpretation, the English version shall be valid for the Parties hereto.

如因翻译而出现解释上的差异时，双方应以英文文本为准。

Actual names and specifications of Products are shown in Appendix 1.

产品的名称、规格详见附录 1。

Details of the information offered by Party B to Party A are shown in Appendix 2.

乙方向甲方提供的资料详见附录 2。

The Appendices attached hereto are made an integral part of this Contract and are equally binding on both parties.

本合同所有附件作为本合同不可分割的组成部分，对双方具有同等约束力。

The annexes as listed in Articles 19 this Contract shall form an integral part of this Contract.

本合同第 19 章列出的附件为本合同不可分割的组成部分。

第四章　工作报告

工作报告是对决策制定过程中所依据的现状、经验和事实的有组织的客观陈述。工作报告中所陈述的事实必须与事件、条件、质量、进展、结果、问题或提议的解决方案有关、帮助当事人了解复杂的商业情况、计划进程、解决问题，使当事人就一系列事件做出决策。这种报告必须基于已经经过证实的事实、所有报告的有效性都是根据这些事实而定，它们是决定未来计划或行动的根本。

按照报告的目的来分类，商务工作报告可分为两种：例行报告（routine reports）和特殊报告（special reports）。常见的形式有调查报告（investigation reports）、市场报告（market reports）、预算报告（budget reports）、进展报告（progress reports）、可行性研究报告（feasibility reports）等。工作报告也可以按照文体色彩分为非正式报告（informal reports）和正式报告（formal reports）。正式报告一般遵循严格的格式要求、长度可以达到几十页甚至更多。正式的报告使用比较正式的文体，通过使用被动语态、名词短语、准确数字、复杂句等的使用得以体现。

一般来说，工作报告的格式和版式均需遵守一般的惯例。正式工作和商务报告大多由标题（title）、综述（executive summary）、受委托事项（terms of reference）、调查方法和程序（method and procedure）、调查结果（findings）、结论（conclusions）、建议（recommendations）、附录（appendices）等部分组成，有时也会有增删调整。

一、工作报告的标题部分

报告的标题应该准确、客观，一般由名词短语构成或直接写成“WORK REPORT”、“A REPORT ON THE OIL TRADE IN IRAQ”等。对于标题的翻译，一般直译就可以了，不必讲究太多的渲染和技巧，关键是让读者一目了然，得其要旨。

二、工作报告的综述部分

一份正式且篇幅较长的报告通常要在报告的签名加上综述。综述一般不超过一页，是对整篇报告的内容概述。综述里的时态用一般时，其中数据可以不太具体，因为正文中有详细说明。例如：

The purpose of this report was to find a suitable warehouse in the Beijing region for our American partner. The team spent one week, and found three possibilities, two situated in Tianjin and the third in Beijing.

The three common bonded warehouses are all satisfactory in terms of warehouse conditions and management level. The area of each warehouse meets the set requirement of 1000－1500 sq. m. in space. In addition，control of the temperature and relative humidity is also standardized.

If any of the two options in Tianjin is chosen，the advantage will be closeness to the port. But the Representative Office of the American partner is based in Beijing，and there will be the question of distance for the management. If Beijing is chosen，transportation and communication expenses between Tianjin and Beijing will then have to be assessed first.

注意，“possibility”的词义在英文中非常抽象，译成中文时可以具体说成“三个备选仓库”，使意思更加明确。“two situated in Tianjin”和“the third in Beijing”，属于英文中的独立主格结构，在翻译时，不要拘泥于原文的结构，在汉语中可以考虑单独成句。“bonded warehouse”是国际贸易领域的一个专业术语，表示“保税仓库”，其中“bonded”是保税之意，又例如：“bonded area”（保税区），“bonded goods”（保税货物），“bonded factory”（保税工厂），等等。“the question of distance for the management”这一句应采取意译的方法，翻译成“管理不方便的问题”。英语因隐去主语或为了显得正式，多用被动语态，如“transportation and communication expenses between Tianjin and Beijing will then have to be assessed first.”，但译成汉语时，为了符合汉语的表达习惯，很多时候最好译成主动语态。

上例的参考译文如下：

本报告的目的是为我们的美国合作伙伴在北京地区找到一个合适的仓库。该组人员耗时一星期，共找到三个备选仓库，其中两个位于天津，一个位于北京。

这三个保税仓库的状况和管理水平都令人满意，每一个仓库的面积也都达到了预定的1000—1500平方米。而且，对温度和相对湿度的控制也符合标准。

如果选择天津，那么优势是靠近港口。但是，美国合作方的代表处设在北京，所以存在着管理不方便的问题。如果选择北京，那么首先不得不考虑天津与北京之间的运输通讯费用等问题。

三、工作报告的受委托事项部分

这部分内容通常用来阐述报告的意图或者主题，包括呈送的对象、提交的时间等等，也可以扼要地说明一下报告的背景。内容通常比较简练。例如：

It is requested on April 10, by the directorate who asked the Personnel Department to investigate the possibility of the firm working “flexitime”, and to make a report on the findings.

4月10日，董事会要求人事部对实行弹性上班制的可能性进行调查，并将结果做一份报告。

这是可行性报告的第一部分。英语中，it is... that... 这样包含主语从句的被动结构很常见，翻译时，一般按照汉语习惯，译成主动语态。由于原文英语中有一个定语从句，定语部分较长，为了汉语译文的美观，可以考虑译成两个句子。“directorate”意为“董事会”，也可以叫作“board of directors”。现在，补充几个公司中常见的组织部门的中英文对照名称：

the General Meeting：股东大会

the Supervisory Committee：监事会

the Strategic Planning Committee：战略规划委员会

the Audit Committee：监事会

the Nomination, Remuneration, and Review Committee：提名、薪酬与考核委员会

Personnel Department：人事部

General Affairs Department：总务部

General Accounting Department / Financial Department：财务部

Sales Department：销售部

Sales Promotion Department：促销部

International Department：国际部

Export Department：出口部

Import Department：进口部

Public Relations Department：公关部

Advertising Department：广告部

Planning Department：企划部

Research and Development Department：研发部

四、工作报告的调查方法和程序部分

这部分主要用来说明收集信息或资料的方法和程序。这部分内容的目的和作用是增强报告的真实性和客观性，尤其是意见调查报告。当然，并非所有报告都需要收集材料，所以不是一切报告都包含次项内容。这部分内容在整篇报告所占的篇幅也较短，往往写成一个自然段。例如：

The Retail Trade Manpower Survey is conducted every two years to collect data on current manpower situation in order to project future manpower requirements and training needs of the industry. Out of the 45，034 registered companies in the retail industry，640 companies were selected by a stratified random sampling method across 13 branches for the survey.

零售业人力调查每两年进行一次，目的是搜集该领域最新人力数据，从而预测未来的人力和培训需求。调查采用分层随机抽样法，从零售业13个类别45034家注册公司中选出640家作为调查对象。

报告中“to collect data on...”是句中的目的状语，因此在译文中加上“目的是”，会使中文显得连贯。“project”在句中是动词，意思是“基于数据进行分析并做出预判”，因此可以考虑译为“预测”。“Out of the 45，034 registered companies in the retail industry，640 companies were selected by a stratified random sampling method across 13 branches for the survey.”这是一个长句。英语经常使用定语从句或后置定语等手段将多个含义写在一个句子中，因此，在翻译成汉语时，为了语句通顺，多采用拆句法和增译法等方法，意思会更加明确。“调查采用分层随机抽样法”“选出640家公司”。

五、工作报告的调查结果部分

工作报告的调查结果就是如实记录所发现的事实，这是报告建立的依据，翻译过程中，要注意内容需准确无误，结构清晰，语言流畅连贯。例如：

> The Government has been vigorously promoting Hong Kong as Asia's World City and shoppers' paradise through the development of different market regions. The strong growth in inbound tourists also helps boost the retail recovery. Total visitor arrivals for 2004 made new record to reach some 21.8 million. It represented an increase of 40.4% on last year，with all market regions showing double-digit growth. Visitors from Chinese mainland have increased most significantly，with arrivals reaching 12.2 million，+ 44.6% on

2003. Mainland visitors accounted for 56% of total arrivals in 2004. The surge in mainland visitors will continue with the opening up of more cities under the "Individual Visitor Scheme."

上例的参考译文为：

政府一直大力将香港作为亚洲国际都会和购物天堂进行推广，并积极拓展不同市场。访港旅客大增亦加速零售业复苏。2004 年抵港旅客达到创纪录的 2180 万人次，较前一年上升 40.4%，与此同时所有市场均呈现两位数增长。其中内地旅客急增至 1220 万人次，较 2003 年上升 44.6%。2004 年访港的大陆游客人数占到了综述的 56%。随着"个人游"计划扩大至内地其他省市，内地游客人数将会持续增加。

"The Government has been vigorously promoting Hong Kong as Asia's World City and shoppers' paradise through the development of different market regions."一句中，"through"引导的状语部分，在译成汉语时可以译成一个小句，其中"development"采取转换法进行翻译，由名词转化为动词。"Total visitor arrivals for 2004 made new record to reach some 21.8 million."和"It represented an increase of 40.4% on last year, with all market regions showing double-digit growth."这两句话，合并成一句话更加符合汉语的表达习惯。"+ 44.6% on 2003"一处反映了英文商务报告简介的一面，在翻译成汉语时，要根据汉语的上下文译成完整句子。

以下为报告这部分的常见句型：

It was found / discovered that... （调查/研究发现……）

It was generally the case that... （通常情况是……）

The major findings of the present investigation can be summarized as follows... （本调查的主要发现可以归结为如下几方面……）

A doubled in （time） compared with those in (time) . （相比之下，A 的时间翻了一倍。）

A in (place) in (time) is... in contrast to... in (place) in (time) . （A 在时间和地点上与……形成对比。）

六、工作报告的结论部分

工作报告的结论部分是写报告的人在报告调查结果的基础上对调查结果进行总结的解释。同一调查结果会因为撰写者的不同而得出不同的结论，但这部分不应当包括报告前文中没有提到的新信息。例如：

The market is slow but competition is pressing. Even when our sales dropped, there is evidence showing that our products still have a good share as we have had many established clients and distributors. If we could provide strong support and better after sales service we might survive the overstressing market competition.

市场疲软但竞争激烈。虽然我们的销售下滑了，但有证据表明，由于我们拥有许多固定的客户和分销商，所以仍占有相当大的市场份额。如果我们能提供有力的支持和更好的售后服务，我们依然可以在激烈的市场竞争中存活下来。

上述报告中“slow”不应译为缓慢，而是商务英语专业表达法，应译为“市场不活跃”或“市场疲软”。“Even when our sales dropped, there is evidence showing that our products still have a good share as we have had many established clients and distributors.”一句中，“share”表示市场份额，但“good share”不应译为“良好的市场份额”。“good ”此处意为“large in amount, size, range”等，所以，应译为“相当大的市场份额。”另外，汉语习惯于先交代原因，再叙述结果，所以，在翻译的时候，应将“as”引导的原因状语从句前置。“distributor”表示分销商，营销领域相关的词还有“wholesaler”（批发商）、“retailer”（零售商）、“agent”（代理商）、“middleman”（中间商）、“after sales service”（售后服务），等等。

七、工作报告的建议部分

建议往往是许多商务报告写作的最重要部分。一份报告有效程度常常取决于报告中所提供的建议质量的高低。建议部分主要内容为报告撰写人在经过充分的论证后认为应当采取的措施或行动。报告人有时也会描述采取措施后可能出现的后果或情形。例如：

Recommendations

1. A traveling sales representative is positioned in Beijing as this man will keep contact with customers who have moved out of Beijing but may still purchase our goods.

2. Beijing Branch needs technical support in dealing with information or data sorting.

3. Replacement should be made in supply with latest models.

建议

1. 在北京设立流动销售代表一名，其职责为与已迁出北京的客户保持有效联系，因为他们可能仍然会购买我们的产品。

2. 北京分部需要技术支持，以有效进行资料信息的处理。

3. 将产品更新为最新款式。

上述报告的第一句话是个长句，应采用拆句法进行翻译，并且要注意各部分之间的语义逻辑关系，必要的时候进行意译。英文正式文件中多用被动句，但汉语中并不多见，因此，在“is positioned”译成主动语态，会更符合汉语习惯，应译为“设立一名流动销售代表”。“as this man will keep contact with customers”这个从句在句中表示原因，但译成工作职责，显得更加流畅，而可以考虑不拘泥于英文的逻辑，因为译成原因状语，此处汉语不如工作职责显得顺畅。“who”引导的定语从句，最好分成两个分句翻译。“in dealing with...”本来在句中只是修饰“support”，说明“support”的内容，在翻译时，可以将它用来表示目的。英语名词动词化使用较多，也就是用名词来表示一个动作的意思，如文中的“replacement”。这是，一般情况下，要按照汉语的习惯，将这类词所表达的动作含义用动词表示出来，所以，译成“将产品更新为最新款式”。

第五章　会议速记

一、速记

一般情况下，人们在会议报告、演讲、座谈、议事、汇报中都可能接触到速记工作，要完整、准确地记录会议内容，留下与会者自身风格的讲话记录。会议结束后，即可整理形成会议发言的相关文字资料，在国际会议中对于一些重要领导人的讲话可立即归档保存，甚至可编辑或编译后马上见报发表。

谈到会议速记，很多人脑海中出现的往往是传统手写模式的一套与母语毫无关系的速记系统编码或符号，需要有速记专业人士花一定的时间将速记编码和符号进行解码方可被非专业人士阅读。此处涉猎的会议速记方法，即“speedwriting-outline”和“quick-notes”模式的速记，不完全是传统意义上的速记法（shorthand，即系统而完整的编码），而是一种开放的，由符合语言表达规律的 LEGO 式[①]速记符号组成的速记法。

当速记将所记录的信息提炼到用少量速记符号加以存载，真正能够吸纳实质语意内容的只有代表词语意义的符号了。“speedwriting-outline”和“quick-notes”模式的速记法包括符号、符号组合及空间配置等。依托各类速符的信息内涵及其之间的结构关系，构建一个与源语信息意义及功能对应的言语结构。一般来讲，与源语在语音、词汇、语法等方面的相似程度越高，就越需要在速记笔记上保留语音、词汇及语法上的特征，否则速记笔记适用程度大大降低。

① LEGO 式：富有创造性的、想象力、可不断拆解重构的。

速记笔记的速符形式包括词语（含缩略语）、图形、数字、线与面的配置，其中前三项常常用来顶代言语中各类词汇，如高频词汇[①]、专有名词[②]、数量词等；线与面的配置在于显示言语的变化，或区分言语段落等。缩略语是有效提升信息记载的最主要手段，包括：词汇类（lexical abbreviation）、文法类（grammatical abbreviation）和文体类（stylistic abbreviation）。针对速记笔记信息速符的形式表征，根据其属性与功能可分为：词语速符（具有实质意义，以实体词为主，如名词、动词等）、会意速符[③]（表抽象语意，以不具备实质意义的功能词为主）、关系速符（语法意义为主）、区别速符（显示信息间的群组关系）。

从一般速记笔记语料可以看到：笔记信息取舍通常是以句子为单位的，与源语的词义、逻辑、顺序、结构等，呈现井然有序的对应关系。词语速符一般都偏重源语，使得速记笔记的记载保持与源语的次序和内容基本上一致。

速记笔记符号多以文字缩略（缩写省略）和符号顶代（顶替取代）为主，组成的基本方式包括：

---

① 高频词汇宜与语境保持紧密关联，如以日本为主题时，才以“J”顶代“Japan”，有效连接信息意义。

② 专有名词的对应速符更要对应明确以便记得准确。此外，对于特定主题下的专有名词（如中国 PRC 等）运用的是基于形象图式的原理，为后期解码时投射还原为源语信息内容做的缩减化。

③ 会意速符（如图示图像符号）与词语速符所不同的是，它脱离源语形式，即不依附于词语的形式和读音，并传达偏于思维化、抽象化的信息概念。会意速符在英语速记者实际操作时是比较普遍的，且似乎颇具共性。

单词字母缩略速记示例

组成方式	速符	意义
前位（首）字母	LPG	liquefied petroleum gas
	OIP	oil in place
	PVT	power—volumn—temperature
	API	Ameriacan Petroleum Institute
首尾字母	wk	week
	tk	tank
	rm	room
省略元音	ppl	pipeline；pipe-laying
	dpp	drillpipe
	gsl	gas oil
	krs	kerosene
省略不发音的字母	no	know
	lit	light
语音顶代	jj	judge
	kas	case
	aj	age
词缀缩形	^{d}ma /^{d}apr /^{d}prv	dismay / disappear / disprove
	^{t}prt /^{t}fr /^{t}mt	transport / transfer / transmit
	pa^{m}/ dev^{m}/ invl^{m}	payment / development / involvement
	ps^{b}/ avl^{b}/ acs^{b}	possible / available / accessible
词缀连带	c/f-ism (zm)	capitalism / feudalism / fascism
	pl/gs/lq-tion (ʃn)	pollution / gasification / liquefaction
语法功能顶代	□ ing /ed	developing country / developed country
原音顶代	gepl	geopolitical
	scs	success
	xtnsv	extensive
约定俗成	TV	television

注：单词字母缩形速记指取词的某部分为速符，储存记录该词的全体意义。
原音顶代中的速记符号以语音特征的方式，顶代该词的全体语音。

标点符号速记示例

组成方式	速符	意义
顶代实词	:	go over/review say / speak / talk / mark / announce / declare
	?	question / problem / difficulty / dilemma
	‘ ’	repeat / retell / mean / define
顶代虚词	…	and so on / and so forth / etc.
	&	and / together with / along with / further more
	( )	among / within / in / inside
	x !	by no means

数学符号速记示例

组成方式	速符	意义
意义顶代	5. 1	Labor Day
	2 bu	mutual supplementation
	2□	both countries
	+	and / besides
	≠	be not / be different from / not so / not same
语音顶代	4u	for you
	3ku	thank you
	9s	nice
	b4/4cst/4tl	before / forecast / foretell

汉语速记数字速符规则列举

500’ (5’)	5, 000′ (5′)	50, 000 w (5w)	5, 000, 000 (5′w)	500, 000, 000° (5°)

图示图形符号速记示例

组成方式	速符	意义
功能图示	∵　∴	due to/by virtue of；hereby/thereof
	≥　≤	more / larger than ；less / smaller than
	—— （熟知语句省略）	Early birds——（Early birds catches worms.） All for one——（All for one，one for all.） A bird in hand——（A bird in hand is worth two in the bush.）
象形图示		"ipad/ipod/apple/achievement/result（…果）
		underground / subway / metro
绘意图示		kindness / friendliness / help / aid
	△；△°	place；local people
	O；O¥；Oy	entire / whole / all；common interests；every year
	☆	important / best / outstanding / brilliant
	∞	connection / communication / relationship
	Ⓘ；Ⓟ	self-centered；people-oriented
		China National Chemical Construction Company merged into and became a subsidiary

中式缩略速记示例

组成方式	速符	意义
拼音缩略	SHD (shd)	Shandong (山东)
	XZ (xz)	Tibet (西藏)
	ZHY (zhy)	CNOOC (中海油)
	cysh	Christmas tree (采油树)
拼音顶代	yfl 或 A^3	Asia, Africa & Latin America (亚非拉)
	ju	chrysanthemum (菊花)
	xie	appreciate / thank; harmony / harmonious (和谐)
	… zu	ethnic group / minority (…族)
	2z	World War II (第二次世界大战)
	m(框内)	domestic residents / country people
同音异体字合体字顶代	吕 (=旅)	travel / tour / trip
	囻	national / domestic residents / country people
	亼	group / community / collective
汉字偏旁部首顶代	宀	room / house ; home / family
	廴	build / construct / set up / establish
	氵	ocean / sea / river / stream / lake / water
	卩	department / division / section

注：古字“囻”（= 国）的新用，作为顶代速符。

类似“亼”（集）简单的异体或合体字顶代速符（包括自创的简化字）仅供个人速记时使用，如给他人识读，建议遵守汉字速符统一书写规范。

各类形式的顶代多是基于人们联想的产物，取决于人们对语言知识掌握程度、文化交流理解水平、工作生活经验积累，等等。前述各类方式的组合混搭在 speedwriting-outlines 和 quick-notes 速记笔记中更是常见的，如英汉混搭、图文混搭、符号混搭等等，其核心目标要达到音落意存效果，最终形成综合式速记笔记（可含提纲式速记笔记）。例如：

quick-notes（**源语信息诠释性速记**）	
现场速写笔记	会后整理提纲
Entre. Prcs 1. idtfy prblm 2. thnk sl$^{\int}$n 3. prpr bsn pln (eqip^{mt}, lc$^{\int}$n, fnc^{ng}, mrkt^{ng}) 4. entre tm (√prsn) 5. tst mrkt^{ng} (sll^{ng} smpls) 6. rs cptl (prds, sll prdcts/ srvcs in lrg qtts)	Entrepreneurial process 1. identify a problem 2. think of a solution 3. prepare a business plan (equipment, location, financing, marketing…) 4. put together an entrepreneurial team (right person) 5. test marketing (selling samples) 6. raise capital (to produce, to sell products/ services in large quantities)

讲话原文：

I want to move on now and take a look at entrepreneurial process. There are six basic steps that most entrepreneurs follow when they start their business. In the first step, they identify a problem, in other words they see a need or a problem that no one else sees. Then in the second step, they think of a solution—what needs to do to solve the problem or meet the need. I think we have already seen several examples today of people who saw a need or an opportunity and then came up with a creative solution to the problem. Step three is to prepare a business plan. A business plan, this means looking at things like equipments, location, financing, marketing and so on. There are thousands of details to think about when you start a new business. As a result, this stage can take a month or even years. The next step, the fourth step is putting together an entrepreneurial team, in other words, hiring the right people to work with entrepreneur in the new business. After that, the fifth step is something called test marketing. That is test marketing. This involves making and selling a small amount of product or service. And if customers like the product or service, then finally entrepreneurs go to the sixth step which is raising capital. Now in this case, capital does not mean a city, it means money. It is another word for money. The entrepreneur has to raise a lot of money in order to produce and sell the product or service in large quantities.

<table>
<tr><th colspan="2">quick-notes（源语信息诠释性速记）</th></tr>
<tr><td>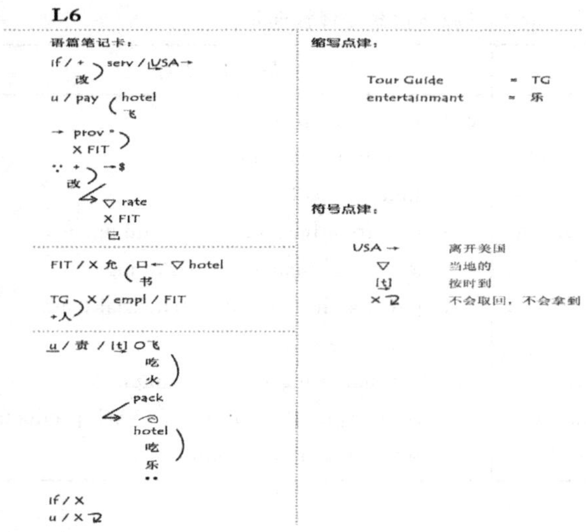
</td>
<td>原文：
Should you wish to add or change services after the departure from the USA, you must pay directly to the service provider such as the hotel or airline, not to FIT Tours. The cost of any changes or additions will be at the local rate at the time of the amendment, not per the FIT Tours brochure, and must be borne by you. ...</td></tr>
</table>

正像中国文献信息速记学会专家顾问白介夫所指出的：“速记的重要性不仅仅在于它是语言学的一个分支学科，或者是作为快速记录语言的一种技能。广泛地讲，应当把速记学作为一个国家、一个民族文化的组成部分。”① 掌握速记就是掌握一种财富，因为它不仅是一种商业或其他社会领域中有用的工具，也是人类精神文化的一个重要成就。速记笔记符号既具有显性文化特征（语言、行为），也具有隐性文化特征（信仰、价值观）。相比较而言，正是因为各类形式的顶代来自于人们的联想，此类速记符号的民族文化特征表现得更为显著。例如：

---

① http：//baike. baidu. com/view/17147. htm.

非英语为母语的速记者有时会借助其母语完成各自的速记笔记

汉式缩略顶代（母语为汉语）	日式缩略顶代（母语为日语）	俄式缩略顶代（母语为俄语）
☺ ke=be interested in the subjects	バイト=part-timer	СЭЗ=economic zone
□ 团=unite our country	リハビリ=rehabilitation	AB=aircraft carrier
n 饣=natural food	ファミレス=family restaurant	НВЭ = for example / for instance

即使相同的民族与文化，也会因生活地域和工作环境不同、学习经历和知识结构差异、年龄性别和性格职业不一样而形成不同的速记笔记习惯与符号风格，因此，“speedwriting-outlines”和“quick-notes”速记笔记符号体系是开放的，始终处于生产中和创造中，并融入一定的个性特征。

此外，网络语言中一些有益于提高速记速度和有效保留意义的网词（“mm”替代“ladies”“girls”“female”“women”）以及部分编制技巧和手段，如旧词新义：instant 后接 star 表“一举成名的明星”、后接 poetry 为“即兴诗歌”、后接“team”即“临时拼凑的球队”；数字密码“U100”为“You are perfect”；“1357”为“odd/strange”（“奇数”和“奇怪”）；同音顶代“CU”为“see you”；“U2”为“you too”等可在速记时采用。1982 年 9 月，美国卡耐基一梅隆大学的斯科特一法尔曼（Scott Fahlman）教授在电子公告板，第一次输入了 ASCII 字符：“：-)”。人类历史上第一张电脑笑脸就此诞生。从此，网络表情符号在互联网世界风行，为社会广泛接受，亦有移入速记笔记符号体系的态势。

由于人们正常书写速度一般比人们讲话语速和思维速度缓慢，结果常常是听的多、想得快、记的少、漏的多，笔头跟不上口头、跟不上思路，更不用谈用纸笔速记了。所以，做好会议速记笔记符号的编制应遵循以下原则：缩略原则（brief forms)，缩略常用而熟知并有规可循的词或句。简易原则(simplification)，简单易写的速记笔记符号节省时间提高工作效率。可识原则（recognition)，速记笔记符号应便于认读，为了增强符号的表意能力，区分某些同音词，应当固定最常用的词语形式。联想原则（association)，速记笔记符号若便于联想通常能有较长的生命力，笔记符号三至五年之后，仍可被认读。

二、会议速记的准备阶段

（一）相关知识与技术技能准备

1. 审读标题。

在会议之前认真审读标题，可以对报告主题有所了解，还可以围绕主题对正文内容进行逻辑推理，做出合理的预测，增加实听时的熟悉感，帮助放松心态，发挥最佳听力水平。例如报告“Facing the Energy Challenge”，标题中提出讨论的主题是“energy challenge”，读者很容易提出问题：能源危机是什么呢？为什么会产生能源危机呢？再看关键词“facing”，即“应对”，我们可以做如下的预测：会议报告人在厘清“能源危机”的概念、原因和后果之后，一定会重点阐述应对措施，还可以进一步深入思考：谁的应对措施？政府？企业？消费者？什么样的应对措施？节能减排？探索新能源？提高能源加工技术？围绕主题提出一系列相关问题之后，听者对会议报告应该不会再感到陌生了，对听会议报告的恐惧感也会减弱，反而对正文内容充满期待。在听会议报告的过程中，一旦预测被一一验证，听者的成就感越来越强，对信息的破译能力也会发挥到最好。

2. 掌握抓准主题句、理清报告脉络的技巧。

主题句（topic sentence）是一段讲话中重要的主旨句子，是“纲”。它说明报告人的中心思想和做报告的目的。报告主题句连接所有支持句（supporting sentences），使它们成为一个有机的整体，有理有据地阐明报告人的观点。主题句可以暗示报告人可能展开的思路与方向、涉及的内容等。以听说为信息交流模式的报告，绝大多数报告人的主题句都出现在比较容易吸引听众注意，或容易给他们留下深刻印象的段首里，有助于迅速引导听众掌握信息和理解其内容。下面，从报告“The Energy Roadmap — Setting the Direction for 21st Century Energy”中节选一段论述为例：

> The first of the five major shifts that have brought us to where we are today is the changing nature of demand for energy. The growth in non-OECD demand has been much sharper that many forecasters projected. Earlier, I said that the non-OECD world now consumed 56% of the world's energy. Not surprising, you may say, but the pace with which that demand has grown has been

extraordinary. In fact non-OECD demand was only 30% of the total in 1970 and since then it has more than quadrupled, consistently exceeding forecasts. Conversely, demand in the older economies of the OECD has slowed more rapidly than many expected. Its highest level on record was in 2007 and it has fallen in four out of the last five years. But looking ahead, because of non-OECD demand, our projection of the most likely outcome is that global consumption of energy will rise by another 30 billion barrels of oil equivalent—or 36%—from 2011 to 2030.

很容易判断出该部分论述的主题句即是首句，简明直接地点出论述的主题——能源需求的变化属性（changing nature of demand for energy）。报告人在之后用摆数据、作对比的方式对“变化”进行阐述。抓住主题句后，即使后段信息中的一大堆数据（百分比、数量、年代）和对比句型跟不上、听不清楚，也不影响此部分报告大意的判断。

3. 捕捉信息。

养成勤做笔记习惯，提高善于提取关键词，抓住重点信息的能力。这里我们讨论的关键词（key words）不同于图书馆学中信息索引的“关键词”，而是包含如下两项内涵：一是在语篇中体现各种逻辑意义和连句手段逻辑信号词；二是提示文章重要信息的实义词。会议报告中常用的逻辑信号词有表示列举关系、增补关系、顺序关系、序列关系、解释强调，归纳总结、转折关系、对比关系、因果关系、确认和条件关系等，具体如下：

表示列举关系的信号词如：take... as an example，for example，for instance，such as，to illustrate，just as，like。

表示增补关系的信号词如：also，namely，and，not only... but also，and as well，furthermore，one more thing，and then，in addition，similarly，as well as，in addition to that，besides，in particular，both... and...，too，either，likewise，what's more，even，moreover。

表示顺序关系的信号词如：after，between，after this/that，earlier/later，afterwards，finally，as，as soon as，initially，at the moment，before，just as，meanwhile，since，until，next，subsequently，when，then，whenever，previously，finally。

表示序列关系的信号词如：for a start，to begin with，for one thing... for another，in the first/second/third place，firstly/secondly/thirdly，last but not least。

表示解释或强调的信号词如：actually，in particular，probably，another way of，refer to，approximately，mainly，slightly，mean，specially，equally，more/most importantly，strikingly，especially，namely，that is，by... I mean，in other word，put it simply。

表示归纳和总结关系的信号词如：accordingly，so，admittedly，thereby，as a result，therefore，basically，in that case，thus，eventually，consequently，in brief，in summary，in conclusion，in short，to conclude，to sum up，to summarize，in a word。

表示转折或对比关系的信号词如：alternatively，however，on the contrary，although，in contrast，as a matter of fact, in spite of, otherwise, but, rather, by contrast, instead, whereas, compared with, while, despite, nevertheless, yet, even though。

表示因果关系的信号词如：as, for, so, as a result, for this reason, the reason why, because of, hence, therefore, lead to, thus, consequently, owing to, thanks to, due to, since。

表示确认的信号词如：apparently, in general, perferably, basically, obviously, specially, certainly, of course, surely, especially, particularly, undoubtedly, generally speaking, plainly。

表示条件关系的信号词如：considering, if, so that, depending on, provided that, unless, for, providing, whether, given that, regardless of, without。

此外，关键实义词承载了报告重要信息点。这类关键词通常会在报告的主题句（句首）出现，在报告展开的部分会以词汇衔接形式重复出现，比如本词的数次重复，或者以同义词、反义词、上下义词等衍生形式出现。下面，以鲍博·都德利（Bob Dudley）在清华大学关于中国能源未来（China's energy future）的报告中的一段为例：

> The recent history of China is a story of *scale and speed*. China is currently the second largest economy in the world, having recently *overtaken* Japan. It is widely expected to become *the world's largest economy* before 2030. Over the last 10 years, Chinese GDP has almost tripled and its energy

consumption has more than doubled. It has become the world's *largest energy producer*, the *largest energy consumer*, *taking over* from the US, and the *largest aggregate emitter* of energy-related carbon dioxide — according to the International Energy Agency and others. Of course, we appreciate that on per capita basis, China's emissions are still far below those of the US and other developed countries.

主题句提示了本部分的中心思想是描述近年来中国能源业的迅猛发展，关键词即规模（scale）和速度（speed）。下述中这两个关键词没有重现，但报告人多次使用了表示规模大的最高级形式"largest"来支撑其论点，如"the second largest economy""world's largest energy producer""the largest energy consumer""the largest aggregate emitter"；用"tripled"和"doubled"表示数量增加幅度之大；用"overtake"和"taking over"表示和日本和美国的对比。报告中没有明确说出发展速度之快，但对应上述巨大飞跃的时间关键词"over the last 10 years"足以说明一切。

专业性会议报告通常会使用很多专业词汇，如果听者的专业词汇储备不足，那么再多的技巧也只是无本之木，几乎派不上用场。因此，在平时的工作中，还要注意阅读相关专业书刊，收集和积累高频的专业词汇，尽力拓展词汇范围。总之，词汇是王道。

4. 了解会议情况。

了解会议情况包括了解会议性质、目的与主要内容。会议是传达文件还是领导人讲话；是学术报告或是座谈交流；是否提供书面文稿资料或 PPT 演示，等等。了解主持人和发言人及他们讲话的习惯，包括文化背景、单位职务、性别年龄、语调语速、停顿特点、重复频率、方言口音，等等。这将有助于在做会议速记前选择恰当的记录方式，是需要逐字逐句记录，还只是要补充记录；是适合精要记录，或是适合精详记录。进而我们再根据不同的记录要求，自行调用和温习，甚至编创适用的个人速符储备，尤其要注意与会议内容相关且陌生的词语速符编制与熟记。在几个、十几个人共同讨论和研究问题的会议上，有的要在会议结束前得出结论，速记时就要注意：要对时间、地点和人员清楚，发言顺序不可混；对讨论的问题和最后的结论要记录准确。发言人如果引用他人一些条文或著作中的一段话，凡是在会后可以查到原文的，速记时可以省去；讲话人的客套话可以省去；讲话人重复多余的内容可以省去。

（二）相关物质与工作环境准备

用于会议速记的纸不宜太光太薄，纸张大小以方便速记为宜，上端或左端装订；室外记录最好采用硬皮本或文件夹。会议速记首选签字笔或钢笔，确保笔油墨水充裕，可多准备两支。会议速记时尽量避免坐在容易受到干扰的进出口的位子，选择距离讲话人比较近，光线好，能看到讲话人表情（包括 PPT 演示）的位子；注意桌椅搭配得要舒适平稳，有益于确保手腕快速运动的持久性，有效减缓压力和过度疲劳。为了后期整理或解译速符，可采用轻便的、电量充足的、内存较大的录音设备，如录音笔等，辅助完成会议速记。随着科学和信息技术的发展，一些辅助速记的软硬件工具应运而生，有关介绍参见附录 2。

三、会议速记的实施阶段

（一）源语信息速写提纲速记

各种报告会，如学术专题报告、经验交流报告、文件传达报告、调查研究报告等等一般不需要全文逐字逐句地记录，多为“精详”之需，或“精要”之求。“精详”速记指主要内容精确而详细的记录，忽略可有可无或重复的语句；“精要”速记指重点典型精确而突出的记录，省略次要和一般内容。如果已配有讲话稿，则在此基础上只需要补充记录。速写笔记提纲（speedwriting-outlines）速记法适用于此类会议。以下速记笔记以“企业家特点与创业路径”报告为样例展开：

会议现场速记笔记
I. Intrl. eg. JB：Amz. cm（strt ’95，1st lrgst intnt bkstr，120 □s） 2.. entre. def. → prsn strt nw bsn/indstr II. Smlr chrctrstcs 1. hv vst / si optnty （1）JB：1st strt us intnt sllng bks 2. X afrd 2 tk rsks （1）FS：fnd. Fdrl Xprs → dlvr pkgs in US ovr9t III. Bkgrnd diff. 1. edu （1）√edu：JB（Prnctn） （2）X fnsh cllg：BG（Mcrsft）

续表

2. orgn (1) rch fmly: FS (2) imgrnts chrldrn: AG (intl) HUN→US (WWII) 3. kri— (1) strt yng ag. (2) strt aftr ag 40/→ 4. m/f (1) f: DF (FC shps Am + AS) IV. Entre. Prcs 1. idtfy prblm 2. thnk sl ∫ n 3. prpr bsn pln (eqip mt, lc ∫ n, fncng, mrktng) 4. entre tm (√ prsn) 5. tst mrktng (sllng smpls) 6. rs cptl (prds, sll prdcts/srvcs in lrg qtts)
V. Cncl3n entre mst rspct d prsn in US ∵ 1. slv prblm 2. prvd jbs 3. mk lif iser + hpper
缩略速写提示： 1. 元音省略：prsn = person；intnt = internet；slv = solve； 2. 首字母缩写（人名、国名、历史事件、性别等）：JB、HUN、WWII、m/f (male/female)； 3. 首尾字母缩写：nw = new；tm = team； 4. 前位字母顶代：entre = entrepreneur；intr = introduction； 5. 字母组合（前后缀）缩略：location (∫ n)；equipment (mt)；(i) = immigrant 6. 语音顶代：2 = to；9 t = night；us = use；kri— = career；iser = easier；Xprs = Express 7. 语法功能顶代：selling；respected；easier； 8. 简易符号顶代：∵ = because；√ = have/right；X = not；+ = and；/→ = after；□s = countries.

会后整理笔记提纲	逻辑信号词提示
I. Intro 1. Example: Jeff Bezos & Amazon. com (started in 1995, first largest internet bookstore, 120 countries) 2. Definition of Entrepreneur: a person who starts new business / industry	*OK, let's begin by ..., There're two ...*
II. Characteristics 1. Have vision / see opportunity (1) Jeff Bezos: first one started to use internet selling books 2. Not afraid to take risks / to fail (1) Frederick Smith: founded Federal Express to deliver packages in US overnight	*First, ...* *Let's look again at the example of ...* *The other ...* *As an example, let me tell you about ...*
III. Differences in backgrounds 1. Education (1) well educated: Jeff Bezos (Princeton) (2) never finished college: Bill Gates (Microsoft) 2. Origin (1) rich family: Frederick Smith; poor family (2) (children of) immigrants: Andrew Grove (Intel), Hungary → America (after WWII) 3. Career (1) start at young age (2) start at age 40 or later 4. Gender (1) Female: Debbi Fields (Mrs. Fields Cookie, shops all over North America and Asia)	*OK, we've just seen ..., but now let's take a look at ...* *First of all, ...* *some ..., but others ...* *Next* *Some ..., in contract, ...* *In addition, ...* *A great example is ...* *OK, the third difference is ...* *Although ...* *And finally, ...* *for example, ...* *So to conclude this section, ...*

续表

IV. Entrepreneurial process 1. identify a problem 2. think of a solution 3. prepare a business plan (equipment, location, financing, marketing ...) 4. put together an entrepreneurial team (right person) 5. test marketing (selling samples) 6. raise capital (to produce, to sell products/services in large quantities)	*I want to move on now and take a look at the ... There are six ...* *In the first step, ...* *Then, in the second step, ...* *Step three is ...* *The next step, the fourth step, ...* *After that, the fifth step is ...* *finally, ... go to the sixth step, ...*
V. Conclusion Entrepreneurs: most respected people in US, because 1. solve problems 2. provide jobs 3. make life easier and pleasant	*I want to say in conclusion, ...*
会后整理的摘要	
Entrepreneurs are a group of people who start a new business or industry. On one hand, entrepreneurs share two most common characteristics: have vision and are not afraid of taking risks. On the other hand, entrepreneurs have different background, involving education, families, gender and age. However, entrepreneurs starting their business generally follow the process: identify a problem; think of a solution; prepare a business plan; put together an entrepreneur team; test marketing and raise capital. So, in a sense, entrepreneurs should be regarded as cultural heroes. They start with dreams. Through hard-working they solve the problems of our society, create millions of jobs, and make our life easier and more convenient.	

续表

讲话原文
How many of you are familiar with the name Jeff Bezos? Okay, how about amazon. com? Have you heard of that? Well, Amazon. com is the world's first and largest Internet bookstore, and Jeff Bezos is the man who started Amazon. com back in 1995. Five years later, Amazon. com was serving millions of customers in 120 different countries. Amazing, right? And this is the reason why in 1999 Jeff Bezos was selected as Times Magazine's *Person of the Year*. A very great honor. Now, Jeff Bezos is actually not the topic of my lecture today. But he is a perfect example of my topic, which is 'entrepreneurs" . That's entrepreneurs, spelled E—N—T—R—E—P—R—E—N—E—U—R—S. It's a French word, meaning a person who starts a completely new business or industry. Enm, someone who does something no one else has done before or who does it in a completely new way, like Jeff Bezos who started the very first Internet bookstore. Entrepreneurs like Jeff Bezos are very highly respected in American society and I think in many other countries, too. So in today's lecture I want to talk about three things. First, the characteristics of entrepreneurs. I mean, what kind of people they are. Second, the kind of background they come from. And third the entrepreneurial process, that is the steps entrepreneurs follow when they create a new business. Okay, let's begin by looking at the characteristics or the qualities of entrepreneurs. There are two qualities that I think all entrepreneurs have in common. First, entrepreneurs have vision. I mean that they have an ability to see opportunities that other people simply do not see. Let's look again at the example of Jeff Bezos. One day in 1994, he was surfing the Internet when suddenly he had a brilliant idea. Why not use the Internet to sell products? Remember at that time, no one was using Internet in that way. After doing some research, Bezos decided the product he wanted to sell was books. That's how Amazon. com got its start. The other quality that I think all entrepreneurs possess is that they are not afraid to take risks. I mean they are not afraid to fail. As an example, let me tell you about Fred Smith, who founded Federal Express, the company that delivers packages anywhere in United States overnight. Smith first suggested the idea for his

续表

company in a college term paper. Do you know what grade he got on it? A "C", but this didn't stop him, and today his company is worth more than 2 billion dollars, and employs more than 25000 people. OK, we have just seen that all entrepreneurs have at least two important qualities in common. But now let's take a look at their backgrounds. And here we will find lots of differences. First of all, some entrepreneurs are well educated, like Jess Bezos who graduated from Princeton University, but others, like Bill Gates, the founder of Microsoft Corporation never even finished college. Next, some entrepreneurs come from rich families like Fred Smith, the founder of Federal Express. In contrast, other entrepreneurs come from poor families. You may be interested to know, in addition, that many entrepreneurs are immigrants or the children of immigrants. A great example is Andrew Grove, the former Chairman of the Intel computer company who was born in Hungary and came to America as a refugee after World War Two. OK, the third difference is that although many entrepreneurs started their careers at a young age, lots of others don't get their start until age 40 or later. And finally, I think it is important to remind you that entrepreneurs are not always men. A famous woman entrepreneur, for example is Debbi Fields who founded Mrs. Field Cookie Company. You can find her shops in malls all over North America and Asia. So, to conclude this section, you can see that entrepreneurs come from many different backgrounds. I want to move on now and take a look at entrepreneurial process. There are six basic steps that most entrepreneurs follow when they start their business. In the first step, they identify a problem, in other words they see a need or a problem that no one else sees. Then in the second step, they think of a solution what needs to do to solve the problem or meet the need. I think we have already seen several examples today of people who saw a need or an opportunity and then came up with a creative solution to the problem. Step three is to prepare a business plan. A business plan, this means looking at things like equipments, location, financing, marketing and so on. There are thousands of details to think about when you start a new business. As a result, this stage can take a month or even years. The next

续表

step, the fourth step is putting together an entrepreneurial team, in other words, hiring the right people to work with entrepreneur in the new business. After that, the fifth step is something called test marketing. That is test marketing. This involves making and selling a small amount of product or service. And if customers like the product or service, then finally entrepreneurs go to the sixth step which is raising capital. Now in this case, capital does not mean a city, it means money. It is another word for money. The entrepreneur has to raise a lot of money in order to produce and sell the product or service in large quantities. I want to say in conclusion that entrepreneurs like Jeff Bezos are among the most respected people in the United States. They are cultural heroes like movie stars or sports heroes. Why? Because starting with the dream and working very hard, these people created companies that solved serious and important problems. They provided jobs for millions of people and in general their companies made life easier and more pleasant for all of us. If you ever order a book from Amazon. com or eat Mrs. Fields cookie, say thanks to the remarkable people who created these companies.

(二) 源语信息全文诠释速记

在涉及一些重要的中外会谈、领导讲话、司法事项的会议上有全文逐字逐句记录的要求，源语信息全文诠释（quick-notes）速记法适合此类会议。速记时应意群为主，字句结合，做到“手记第一句，脑储第二句，耳听第三句”。就诠释性速记视觉效果而言，一般由上至下的垂直记录能够较好地体现速记笔记所记录信息的逻辑结构。如句法中词语间为并列关系，垂直记录易于体现其排比关系，每行记一个字或一个符号并排的意群含义与逻辑关系会一目了然；若有递进或新意群关系，则可采用缩进模式，简捷清晰。例如：

These documents indicate his/her name, gender, date of birth, nationality, marital status, occupation, nature of the work and the name of the person to marry.

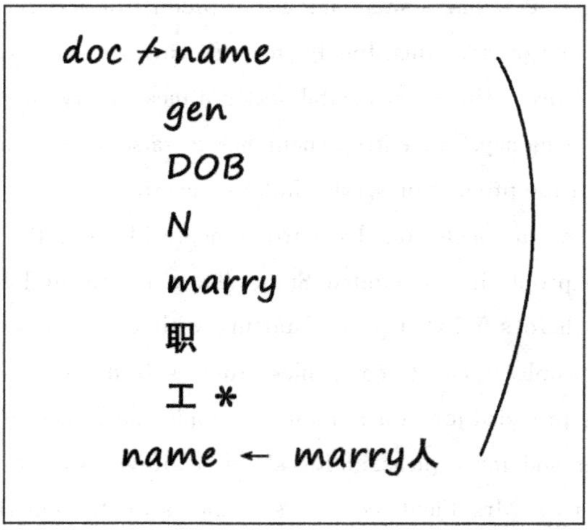

在垂直记录的基础上，当句子具备类似从属关系和主次关系的逻辑含义时，可以通过换行缩进的方式来记录，以获得更清晰的视觉效果。例如：

Calligraphy is understood in China as the art of writing a good hand with brush or the study of the rules and techniques of this art. As such it is peculiar to China and the few countries influenced by ancient Chinese culture.

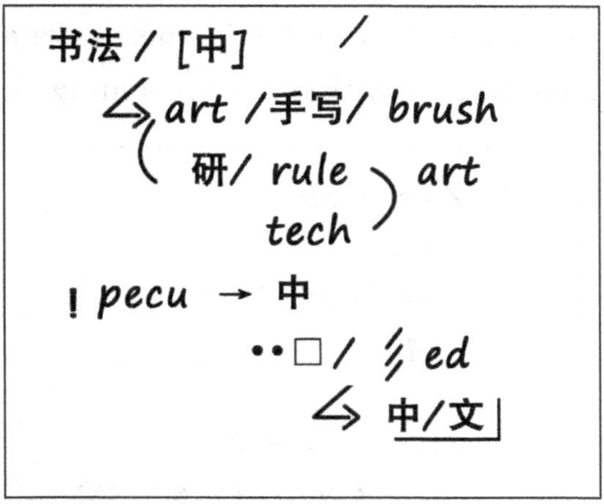

在每段意群结束之处，速记时多以一条横线划开，表示一个语段的结束。一个意群可以是几句话或几段话，也可以是句子片段。一般来讲，两条横线之间的内容包括至少一个内缩式单位。有的速记人员习惯用斜线表示意群的结尾，这也未尝不可，但与垂直和缩进结构形成的对比不如横线鲜明。因为如果需要记录的内容较多，结尾处的标识对于速记人员来说就非常重要，最好能够在尾部采取难以误解的形式标示出来，以便能够在语流结束时快速定位到上一个意群结束和这一个意群开始的位置，特别是在一页当中记录了多个段落的时候尤其重要。例如：

> After defining the accounting elements, let's examine assets, liabilities and owner's equity with accounting equation: Assume that a business owns assets of ＄12,000, borrows from creditor ＄3,000, and that the owner invests ＄9,000. The entries made in the accounting equation would be: Assets = Liabilities + Owner's equity, in numbers, ＄12,000 =

$3,000＋$9,000, right? OK, next, we are going to examine further with other accounting elements.

└ / def / acc ele
ass
lia) acc / equ
equ
e. g.
ass ↗ $ 12000
↗ (cred / $ 3000
own/ $ 9000
acc / equ
└→ ass = lia + equ
$ 12000= $ 3000 + $ 9000
next / + acc ele

由于笔记记录的时间十分有限，一些速记人员则使用目的语完成笔记记录。不过，也有学者认为，在实际速记记录过程中，哪种语言记录对速记者来说更为方便就用哪种。事实上，更多的情况是两种语言都会用到，即“代码混记”（code-mixing）。例如：

Journalists' reporting is a bit like swimming. People say that swimming is the best exercise you can do, because it uses all the different parts of the body. You are using your arms. You are using your legs. You are breathing to move forward. But really, even the muscles of your back and stomach are working too.

Jo / rept ≈ swm
ひと / Q
∟ swm → / exe
∵ use / X = / whl bdy
∠ うで
あし
brth / →
evn / mscl ＋ bck い

由于笔记极具个人特色，而笔记的最终评判标准是能否快速、准确、全面地将信息记录下来。因此，所谓的目的语结构原则，是强调无论是使用源语还是目的语进行记录，都要尽量体现目的语的语法结构和使用习惯，这样才能最大化的加速语言信息的转换，使速记者笔记辨识效果更好。

一般来讲，非文字符号的比重在速记内容中不超过50%。速记时不必特别迷信符号的使用，把大量的时间花在学习别人推荐的各种符号上，这样不仅发挥不了符号的助忆作用，反而会让符号成为笔记的负担和累赘，得不偿失。笔记符号需要有这样的特点：好写，易读，意义明确，一目了然。比如“＝”代表“相等”，“相似”，“相同”；“＜”表示“比…少，弱”“不如…”；“＜＜”表示“比……少得多，弱得多”“远远不如……”；“＊”表示“重要”“关键”；“≈”表示“大约是”“差不多是”。符号无所谓好与坏，只要用起来得心应手就是好符号。每个速记人员都会有自己的代码语库，而更多的是自己创造并熟练使用的。

如在一篇讲话中，某个复杂而重要的概念一再出现，这时，速记时不必每次都把它整个记下来而是找一个“临时符号”代替。例如：在一篇关于“电网设置”的科技专题讨论中，“高压电弧触电”和“低压跨步触电”被一再提及，就可以分别用“G”和“D”来代替。再如，外汇零售业务中“white labeling（白标）”的概念，指外汇零售中包含客户化服务内容的代理业务。每当这一概念被提及时，就可以在笔记上记下“Δ”以代表对白标的专业解释段落，但前提是“Δ”在同一语境中不代表其他含义。

针对数字，尤其是多位数的阿拉伯数字英汉转换记录，最常用的便是“，｜”分割法或称“点三杠四”11。“，”主要是针对英文语境下的多位数，“｜”则针对中文语境下的多位数。在进行数字的听记过程中，可以遵循“听记”、“补零”和“移位”三个步骤。所谓“听记”，就是按照所听语言中对数字的表述顺序进行记录。例如，阿拉伯数字1002193456780，当发言人用英文表述时，他会首先以三位（digits）一个数节（trunk）的方式从右至左用“,”标示在文字中，即1,002,193,456,780，从右往左第一个逗号是“千（thousand）”，第二个逗号是“百万（million）”，第三个逗号是“十亿（billion）”，第四个逗号则是“万亿或兆（trillion）”。那么，发言人会这样读这一数字：“one trillion and two billion one hundred and ninety-three million four hundred and fifty-six thousand seven hundred and eighty”。速记时，本着“听到什么记什么”的原则，将所听到的数字用阿拉伯数字记录下来，在听到trillion，billion，million或thousand的时候，只需划逗号“,”，当感觉不连贯的数字之间，可以留出一定的间隙，留待过后补零。按照这一原则的阿拉伯数字笔记应当是这样的：“1,2,193,456,780”。接下来便是第二步——“补零”。补零也是按照阿拉伯数字本身的习惯，每三位一个数节，将不足三位的数节中空缺的位置以“0”填充。于是，上文中的数字就变为：“1,002,193,456,780”。第三步叫作“移位”，这是英汉互转的关键环节。由于汉语的数字阅读习惯是每四位阿拉伯数字一个数节，因此，需要首先从右至左每四位划一个竖线“｜”，以备汉语读出：“1,｜002,1｜93,45｜6,780”。第一个“｜”是汉语中的“万”，第二个“｜”是“亿”，第三个是“兆”，于是以汉语读出这个数字便为：“一兆零二十一亿九千三百四十五万六千七百八十”。此外，“移位”还有小数点平移的含义，主要是针对可以简化阅读的后几位数字连续为零的整数。比如，“37000000”的英文写法，首先按照三位数分节加上逗号，变为37,000,000，英文阅读为“thirty-seven million”，在“听记”的时候，听到“37”之后，可以划一个逗号“,”然后以“—”代替三个零，于是便可以记录为37,—,—。转换成汉语时，可以仍采用划“｜”的方式，变为37,—｜0,—，然后读为“三千七百万”，也可以通过小数点的平移，设想左边又划了一个“｜”，则可以读为“零点三七亿”。数位之间的转换，则可以通过公式进行记忆：1万＝10 thousand，1亿＝100 million，十万＝100 thousand，百亿＝10 billion，千万＝10 million，千亿＝100 billion。前述内容主要是以听到的数字为英文表述，如果听到的是中文数字，则在“听记”环节采用竖线“｜”进行记录，然后从右至左用逗号“,”划分，再以英文的阅读习惯读出。“补零”和“移位”的方法也与上文中所描述的方法相同。

下面以英国首相戴维·卡梅伦（David Cameron）在2012年冬季达沃斯世界经济论坛年会上讲话为例（时长为3分零7秒），对国际会议速记笔记样例进行解析。

始于2007年的环球金融危机令世界经济持续几年陷入低

迷，2012年的达沃斯论坛便是在这样的环境下举行的，并将主题定为“大转型：塑造新模式”，有分析人士认为，这一主题表明，世界经济论坛充分认识到目前全球各领域存在着深层结构性问题，进行全面深入的变革已不可回避。当年货币基金组织将全球经济增长率和主要经济大国的增长率的期望值下调，只有大概3.3%，欧元区面临更大的窘境，被认为处于经济萧条期。在此次会议上，英国首相卡梅伦向欧洲各国施压，敦促该地区的各国领导人采取更为大胆且决断的行动，来解决该地区的主权债务危机。卡梅伦在讲话中表示，欧洲其他国家应该仿效英国，采取更加切实可行的措施应对危机。卡梅伦在讲话中发出警告称，目前欧洲大陆正面临着十分危险的时刻。

速记从卡梅伦刚一讲话开始，持续3分零7秒结束，现将该部分讲话文本以及相应的速记笔记诠释列于下文：

讲话原文
We meet today at a perilous moment for economies right across Europe. Growth has stalled. Unemployment is rising. The prospect of Europe getting left behind is all too apparent. While China grows at 8%, India at 7% and Africa at 5.5%, the European Commission forecasts the EU will grow by just 0.6 per cent in the whole of 2012 — and even that is assuming the problems in the Eurozone get better not worse. Yesterday in Britain we had the official figures for the final quarter of last year—and they were negative. Other large economies of Europe are forecast to have a similar outcome or worse. In just four years Government debt per EU citizen has risen by 4,500 euros. Foreign direct investment has fallen by around two-thirds. And in more than half of EU Member States, a fifth of all young people are now out of work. So this is not a moment to try and pretend there isn't a problem. Nor is it a moment to allow the fear of failure to hold us back. This is a time to show the leadership that our people are quite rightly demanding . Tinkering here and there

续表

and hoping we'll drift to a solution simply won't cut it anymore. This is a time for boldness not caution. Boldness in what we do nationally — and together as a continent.

In Britain we've had to be bold. We were faced with the biggest budget deficit in our peacetime history more than 10 per cent of our GDP. We had the most leveraged banks, the most indebted households and the biggest housing boom. To be cautious would have been catastrophic.

Instead we were bold and decisive. We formed the first Coalition government for 70 years. We legislated for a fixed-term, five year, Parliament which has helped to give people the confidence of stability and credibility. We put forward an aggressive set of plans to get to our economy back on an even keel. ? 5. 5 billion saved inside the first financial year the one already on the way. Welfare bills — cut. The cost of government — cut. Public sector pay — frozen. The State Pension Age — increased.

Let me give you one example — reform of public sector pensions. This is a difficult issue for any government. We want public servants to have good pensions. We've ensured that's the case but at the same time we've actually cut the long term cost in half.

现场笔记

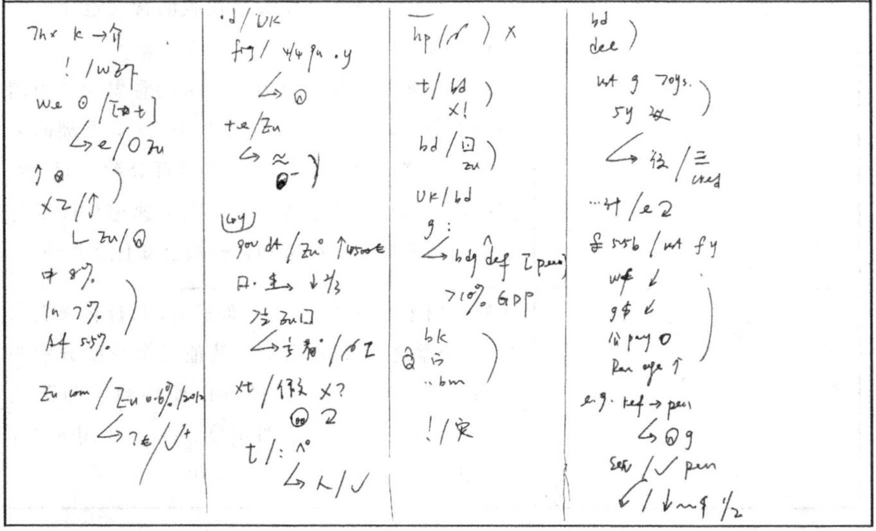

国际会议的讲话具有鲜明的特色——不同的英语口音、语速通常较慢、节奏平稳、专有名词较多、多涉及政治经济领域的内容等等。因此在进行国际会议英语速记的时候，最好预先熟悉发言人的讲话特点以便快速进入速记状态。此外，要根据会议主题，了解相关背景知识和英语专有名词，这样在速记时能够做到心中有数，会放松精神将更多精力投入到速记当中，有时甚至能预知接下来的讲话内容。2012 年达沃斯经济论坛涉及大量经济发展、全球贸易、欧债危机等问题，速记员要根据这个大的背景做好充分地准备。

英国首相卡梅伦在 2012 年达沃斯世界经济论坛年会上的讲话节选速记笔记如上述所示，其中包含了数字、英语字母、英语单词缩写、中文、箭头、各种图形符号等。

数字的记录

中 8% In 7% Af 5.5%	记忆力再好的速记员也不可能保证能够准确地记住数字，因此速记笔记中非常重要的一项为记录数字。数字记录尽量避免单纯地只记录数字，要让数字变得有意义，即数字代表的含义也要一并进行记录。 此处使用的为百分数，表示的意思为“中国的经济增长速度为 8%，印度的为 7%，非洲的为 5.5%”。笔记中只出现了国家和百分数，而“经济增长”的相关符号省略了，因为速记员根据背景知识和记忆看到国家和百分数已知什么意思。
4/4 qu	此处使用了分数 4/4，与后面的 qu 联合起来表示“第四个季度”，以此类推，其他三个季度分别为 1/4qu，2/4qu，3/4qu。还可以使用数字与英文缩写“4th qu”表示第四季度，不过使用 4/4qu 不会出现过多的字母，容易辨识。

续表

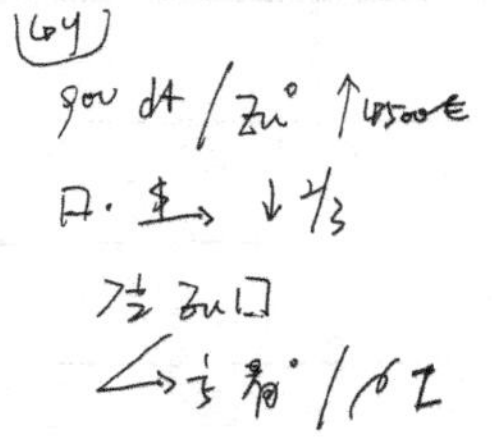	此部分出现的数字较多，“4y”表示4年，用半框括起来表示4年间；“4500”表示4500欧元；其他数字要结合前后笔记方能看出数字代表的意思，分别为“国外投资下降2/3”，“一半以上的欧洲国家”，“1/5的青年”。
>10% GDP	此处表示10%以上的GDP
1st g 70ys. 5y 议)	“1st”表示“第一个”，“70ys”表示“历经70年”，“5y”表示5年制的（议会）。
£5.5b / 1st fy	“£5.5b”表示55亿英镑；“1st”表示“第一个”
公 pay 0	此处的“0”结合其他符号意为“公共支出为零”。
↓ ~ $ 1/2	此处表示“削减了一半的长期费用”，英文原文为“cut the long term cost in half”，英语速记紧紧跟随讲话的发音，因此有时完全使用“顺序驱动原则”，听到什么就直接记录了。

英语字母和单词缩写的使用

Thx K	Thanks Klaus；施瓦布（Klaus Schwab）为达沃斯经济论坛的执行主席（Executive Chairman），是他介绍卡梅伦出场的，因此卡梅伦讲话的首句为“谢谢，克劳斯”。一般而言，在速记中语速较快时，名字通常用首字母来表示。
WEF	World Economic Forum 世界经济论坛
e/O Eu	economy in the whole Europe
Eu com	European Commission
·d	yesterday

续表

fig	figure
·y	last year
gov dt	government debt
xt	not the time
hp	hope
bd	bold；“bold”一词在讲话中反复出现，表达了卡梅伦对于经济要“放手去做，大胆开拓”的主张。
bdg def	budget deficit
bk	bank
bm	boom
dec	decisive
cred	credibility
fy	fiscal year
wf	welfare
e.g.	for example
ref → pen	reform pension
ser	servant

中文或偏旁部首的使用

介	introduction
×工	no work，unemployment
中	China；也可以用 CN 表示中国
青	youngster，the young
假	pretend
人	people
户	house
灾	disaster，catastrophic
议	parliament，discuss，discussion
信	confidence，letter
计	plan
公	public

英语速记主要使用英语单词、缩写或字母，因为听什么记什么是最为方便快捷的。对于中文为母语的速记员而言，有时听到英语单词后会自动地联想到它的中文对应词，也会随手记录下来，尤其是当中文拼写较为简单或者英文缩写容易混淆的时候。上述中文速记符号都比较简单，笔画较少，例如："工"，"人"等，有时还可以使用手写简化字以减少笔画，例如：使用"信"来代替"信"。

图形符号的使用

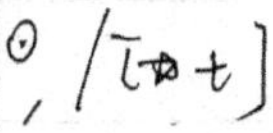	此处符号“⊙”表示“会面（动词）”，符号“☆”表示“重要的”，符号组合意为“在重要的时刻会面”。
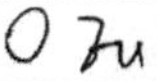	此处符号“○”表示“全部”，符号组合意为“整个欧洲”。
	此处符号“⊗”表示“停止”，符号组合意为“增长停滞不前”。
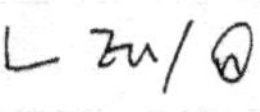	此处符号“└──”表示“将来”，符号“○”表示“悲伤”，符号组合意为“欧洲经济的前景不容乐观”。
	此处符号“⊖”表示“悲伤”，符号组合意为“更为糟糕”。
	此处符号“°”表示“人”，符号组合意为“欧洲人”。
	此处符号表示国外。
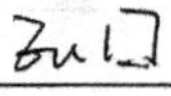	此处符号“□”表示国家，符号组合意为“欧洲国家”。
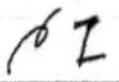	此处符号“/”表示“清除”，符号组合意为“失去工作”。
	此处符号“◎”表示“害怕”，符号组合意为“让恐惧使我们退缩”。
	此处符号“ˆ”表示“最高级，顶点”，符号“°”表示“人”，符号组合意为“领导人”。
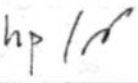	此处符号“/”表示“清除”，符号组合意为“希望问题得以解决”。
	此处符号表示“国内”，在卡梅伦讲话中指的是英国。
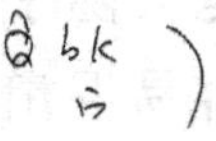	此处符号“⊖”表示“负债的”，符号“ˆ”表示“最高级，顶点”，符号组合在笔记中代替“the most leveraged”和“the most indebted”两个词组，因为两个词组单词在此处意思相近，因此使用同一个符号，与后面的名词组合在一起，意为“举债最多的银行、负债最重的家庭”。在速记当下，时间紧迫，有时不能立即写出听到的单词或想到合适的符号，一些概念比较笼统的符号就非常实用了。“⊖”可以用于表示一切不好的、糟糕的、令人不愉快的感觉，例如：“伤心”、“不满”、“失败”等等。
	此处三道横线的符号表示“稳定”。
	此处符号“⊖”表示“困难的”，符号组合意为“对于政府而言是困难的”。
	此处波浪线符号表示“长期的”。

数学、标点及其他符号的使用

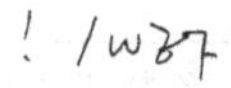	“!”表示感叹或感慨，在笔记中可以代替一系列的单词，此处代替“great”，符号组合意为“再次参加世界经济论坛感觉非常棒”。
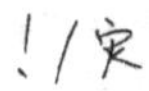	此处的“!”代替“To be cautious”表示“小心谨慎”。
	此处的“!”同样代替“cautious”表示“小心谨慎”，符号组合意为“不应该小心谨慎”。
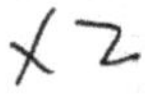	此处符号“×”表示“没有”，符号组合意为“没有工作”。
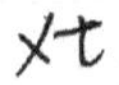	此处符号“×”表示“不是”，符号组合意为“不是…的时候”
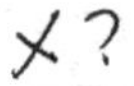	符号“×”和“?”组合在一起意为“没有问题”。
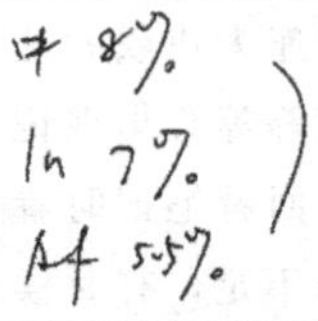	右括号“)”在笔记中的使用非常频繁，他将所有并列的内容括在一起，令笔记条理清楚，逻辑性强。
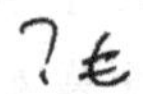	此处的“?”表示“问题”，符号组合意为“欧元区的问题”。
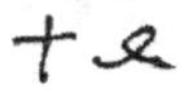	此处的“+”表示“另外，其他”，符号组合意为“其他经济体”。
	此处“≈”表示“类似”。上下文的意思为“其他经济体的情况与英国类似”。
	此处的“−”表示“比较级”。有时候右上角的“+”表示比较级。两个符号的用法略有不同，通常积极肯定的词的比较级用“+”，消极否定贬义词的比较级用“−”。此处符号“⊖”表示“悲伤”，因此比较级使用“−”。

续表

t/:	“:”表示“显示、表明、展现…”，此处符号组合意为“是时候展现…”。
g :	此处的“:”表示“面对、面临…”，符号组合意为“政府面临”。
…计	此处的省略号“…”表示“很多”，符号组合意为“很多计划”。
√+	符号“√”代表的意思比较宽泛，可以表示一切好的东西；符号“+”在此处表示比较级；此处符号组合意为“（情况）变得更好”。
人/√	此处符号组合意为“人们所需要的”。
√ pen	此处符号组合意为“丰厚的退休金”。
—hp/(√) ×	此处包含三个符号，“√”表示“清除、解决”，“×”表示“不可以”，另外还有一个横线符号“——”，该符号表示此处有内容，但是没有记录下来。有时候因为语速太快或者速记者个人原因，例如：走神、超出词汇量范围等等会出现记录空白，如果接着记下面的内容会使速记员在回看笔记时看不出哪里有信息遗漏。用“”可以弥补这样的不足，有时候还可以根据上下文内容，将遗漏的信息大概猜出来。此处未记录的内容为“Tinkering here and there”，这是一个英文词组，字面意思为“修补这里和那里”。这里的符号组合意为“…希望问题会解决并没有用”。

箭头的使用

Thx k →介	此处使用向右的箭头，连接“谢谢”和“介绍”，后者为前者的宾语补足语，省略介词“for”用箭头表示逻辑关系。此处也可以使用“/”来分割意群即可，不用箭头表示逻辑关系。
ref → pen	此处的右箭头连接“改革”和“养老金”，前后构成动宾关系，本属于同一个意群应记在一起，但是两个单词均为英文缩写，放在一起容易混淆，因此用右箭头隔开，并指向改革的内容。

续表

	此处向上的箭头表示“经济增长”，与表示结束的符号一起，意为“经济增长停滞不前”。
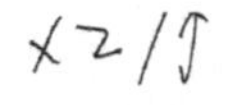	此处向上的箭头与前面符号组合一起，意为“失业率增加”。
	此处向上箭头表示增长 4500 欧元。
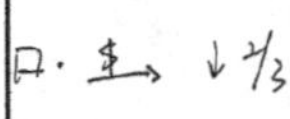	向右的箭头与上面的美元符号组合意为“投资”，此处符号组合意为“国外投资下降 2/3”。
	此处指向左下的箭头表示“削减”，符号组合意为“福利削减，政府支出削减”。
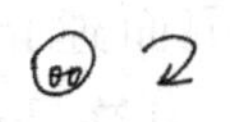	此处从上向下的左拐弯箭头表示“退缩”，与前面符号组合意为“恐惧令人们退缩”。
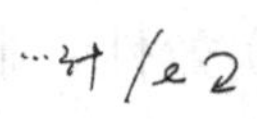	此处从上向下的左拐弯箭头表示“恢复”，符号组合意为“很多计划令经济得以恢复”。
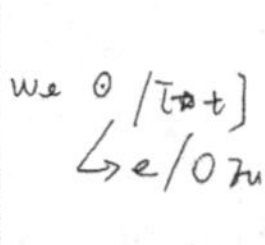	此处从上向下的右拐弯箭头表示上下两行符号存在逻辑关系。箭头的起始点指向的内容“⊙”在下面还要继续说明，即“我们在重要的时刻场合会面，这次会面是为了探讨整个欧洲的经济”。拐弯箭 头承上启下，令笔记逻辑性更强。
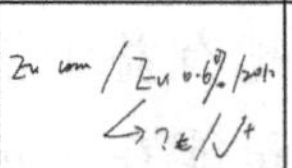	此处的右拐弯箭头将“Eu 0.6%”与下行符号相连，意为“欧洲的增长率为 0.6%，而这个数值还是欧元区情况有所好转的结果”。

上文对卡梅伦讲话节选的速记笔记进行了详解。国际会议速记除了使用英文缩写外，还使用了大量的数字、箭头、数学符号、标点符号以及图形符号等。作为经济类国际会议，包含了很多相关方面的词汇或短语的速记方法，例如：“bk”表示银行、“g”表示政府、“bdg”表示预算、“def”表示赤字、“×工”表示失业、“主,”表示投资、“∧°”表示领导人、“□”表示国家、“回”表示国内、“口.”表示国外以及货币符号＄、

£的使用等等。国际会议场合正式，作为速记员和口译员在速记时要高度集中，对于数字等重要信息千万要记录准确。由于国际会议为现场记录，因此对速记速度也有较高的要求。

四、会议速记的收尾阶段

速记的过程是将口语转换成速记符号为主的书面形式，会后需要进一步解译和整理。速记的根本目的是记录源信息。速记的内容是对源信息内容的采集记录，而不是唯速记而速记，在忠实于源语意义的基础上，解译速记可参照速记笔记符号记录源信息质量基本衡量标准来检查完成速记笔记的实效性；通过补充、调整、删减和改错完成会议记录的最终形式的整理材料。

1. 信息完整性（faithfulness）。

速记笔记符号构成能正确反映所记录源信息的完整性。速记成果的主要目的是获取信息。获取的信息越多，越有益于信息诠释与整理文稿的准确性。速记信息关键词的数量能在一定程度上反映记录源信息的完整性。

2. 逻辑结构性（outlines）。

逻辑结构性是指速记时构建的速记笔记的框架结构。主要体现在速记笔记辅助性结构符号的应用是否能使源信息呈现主次分明、层级清楚。一般结构信号词有助于帮助形成逻辑性强的笔记框架。

3. 笔记诠释性（reformulation）。

笔记诠释性是在对源信息理解的基础上，结合其自己的知识与经验，内化源信息，通过速记笔记重构的方式记录所需转述的信息。

4. 笔记可识率（recognition）。

笔记可识率分个性化可识率和通识化可识率。前者针对个人而言。速记时所形成的速记笔记符号在一定时限内首先应能被其本人识辨（可读），并体现其本人的个性特征。后者针对非个人而言，速记时所形成的速记笔记在一定时限内能被记录人本人以外的人员辨识（可读），并体现民族文化或学科领域等相关特征。

第六章　论坛口译

一、论坛口译概述

（一）国际知名论坛概览

论坛指对公众发表议论的地方，分为实体参与型论坛与网络交流型论坛。实体参与型论坛为各类研讨会与座谈会，英文名称通常为“forum”，有时也可称为“symposium”。网络交流型论坛指各种网站论坛，英文名称为“Bulletin Board System”（电子公告板），简称“BBS”。本章探讨的论坛口译是指各类在固定时间和地点由不同人群参与的国际型座谈和研讨会当中的口译。

1. 最具影响力国际论坛。

（1）世界经济论坛

世界经济论坛（World Economic Forum，官方网站 http：//www.weforum.org）是以研究和探讨世界经济领域存在的问题、促进国际经济合作与交流为宗旨的独立的国际性机构，前身为“欧洲管理论坛”，于1987年更名为“世界经济论坛”，总部设在瑞士日内瓦，每年冬季在瑞士滑雪胜地达沃斯举办的年会而闻名于世，故又俗称“达沃斯论坛”（Davos Forum），年会一般是在1月下旬举行，聚集全球政界、商界、学术界以及媒体人士讨论世界所面临最紧迫问题。每年都要确定一个主题，在此基础上安排200多场分论坛讨论。2015年1月21至24日召开的年会主题为“全球新局势”（The New Global Context）。

（2）博鳌亚洲论坛

博鳌亚洲论坛（Boao Forum for Asia，官方网站 http：//www. boaoforum. org）是政府、企业及专家学者共商经济、社会、环境及其他相关问题的高层对话平台，是一个非官方、非营利性、定期、定址、开放性的国际组织，于2001年召开首次大会，正式成立，总部设在中国海南省博鳌镇。博鳌亚洲论坛以“平等、互惠、合作和共赢”为主旨，立足亚洲，推动亚洲各国间的经济交流、协调与合作；同时又面向世界，增强亚洲与世界其他各地区的对话与经济交往。

（3）《财富》全球论坛

《财富》全球论坛（Fortune Global Forum，官方网站 http：//www. fortuneconferences. com/global-forum）于1995年创办，由美国《财富》杂志主办，邀请各大跨国企业的董事长、总裁、首席执行官等高级管理人士以及世界知名的政治家、政府官员和经济学者等，共同探讨全球经济问题。每16至18个月在世界不同地点举办一次会议，2013年6月6日至8日举行的第12届《财富》全球论坛选址中国成都，主题为“中国的新未来”。该论坛被视为“把握世界经济走向最清晰和最直接的窗口”，影响力不容小觑。

（4）经济合作与发展组织

经济合作与发展组织（Organization for Economic Cooperation and Development），简称经合组织（OECD），由34个国家组成，成立于1961年，总部设在法国巴黎。旨在共同探讨和应对全球化带来的经济、社会和政府治理等方面的挑战，并把握全球化带来的机遇，促进全球贸易的发展。经合组织每年在巴黎举办一次论坛（官方网站 http：//www. oecd. org/forum），聚集工商、政治以及社会其他领域人士共同探讨全球亟待解决的社会与经济问题。2014 年论坛主题为“Resilient Economies for Inclusive Societies”（构建全纳（包容性）社会的弹性经济）。

（5）亚太经济合作组织

亚太经济合作组织（Asia-Pacific Economic Cooperation，APEC，官方网站 http：//www. apec. org）是亚太各地区之间促进经济成长、合作、贸易、投资的论坛，是亚太地区最具影响的经济合作官方论坛，始设于 1989 年，现有 21 个成员经济体，总部设在新加坡。2014 年 APEC 峰会在北京举办，主题是为“共建面向未来的亚太伙伴关系”（Shaping the Future through Asia-Pacific Partnership）。

2. 最具影响力国际能源会议及论坛。

（1）世界能源大会

世界能源大会（World Energy Congress，官方网站 http：//www. worldenergy. org）由世界能源理事会（World Energy Council）主办，每三年举行一次，会期 5 天，是全球能源界讨论能源工业发展的最主要会议。各个能源生产国、消费国、政府、能源相关国际组织和能源企业参加大会，进行讨论和对话，共同应对全球能源问题。第 22 届世界能源大会于 2013 年在韩国大邱举办，大会主题为“保障明日的能源安全”（Securing Tomorrow's Energy Today）。

（2）国际能源论坛

国际能源论坛（International Energy Forum，官方网站 http：//www. ief. org）是世界最大的能源领域的论坛，参加者除了来自国际能源署（IEA）以及石油输出国家组织（OPEC）的成员国外，还来自包括巴西、中国、印度、墨西哥、俄罗斯以及南非等国际上重要能源供需大国，论坛秘书处设于沙特阿拉伯的利雅得。

(3) 世界石油大会

世界石油大会，全称是“世界石油大会——石油科学、技术、经济及管理论坛”(World Petroleum Congresses－Forum for Petroleum Science, Technology, Economics and Management, WPC)，是一个非政府、非盈利、国际性的石油代表机构，被公认为世界权威性的石油科技论坛。世界石油大会1933年8月在伦敦成立，每三年举行一次。

(4) 国际石油周

国际石油周(International Petroleum Week，简称IP week，相关网站 https://www.energyinst.org/events/ip-week)是英国能源研究所(Energy Institute, EI)举办的全球石油天然气企业领导人论坛，每年召开一次，总部设在英国伦敦。2015年2月论坛主题为“Strategies for the changing oil and gas landscape”(如何应对不断变化的石油天然气格局)。

(5) 普氏全球能源展望论坛

普氏全球能源展望论坛(Platts Global Energy Outlook Forum，相关网站 http://www.platts.com/events/2014/globalenergy/index)由普氏能源资讯公司举办，聚集全球能源行业以及能源公司的决策者、管理者以及经营者们以及媒体人士探讨能源问题。普氏能源资讯公司是全球领先的能源和金属信息提供商，为石油、天然气、电力、煤炭、运输、石化和金属行业提供对其业务至关重要的市场新闻和数据、基准估价、新闻简报，同时打造行业领先的会议，帮助客户作出更加明智的贸易和商业决策。普氏能源资讯每年都在美国纽约市举行普氏全球能源奖(Platts Global Energy Award)以及普氏全球能源展望论坛，论坛包括主旨发言(keynote speech)以及专题讨论（panel discussion）。

（二）论坛口译简介

口译（interpretation）与笔译（translation）为翻译活动的两种实践形式。口译即口头翻译；笔译即笔头翻译，又称文字翻译。翻译是对外交流和国际交往的重要桥梁和纽带，为文化传播做出巨大贡献。

在各类国际论坛以及会议上，参加者来自不同的国家和地区，因此在做主题发言和讨论时需要进行大量的口译，针对不同地区的发言人需要不同语种的译员。一般译员能够完成双向口译，例如：英汉、汉英口译，也有个别有能力的译员能够完成三种及以上语种的互译，例如汉英、汉法、英法等。

1. 论坛口译分类。

口译就其工作方式而言一般可分为交替传译（consecutive interpretation）和同声传译（simultaneous interpretation）两大类。

交替传译指讲话与翻译交替进行的口译形式，讲话人说完一段话，讲完一个话题或回答一个问题后停下来，由译员执起话筒现场立即译给听众，如同自己在演讲，也称为即席翻译。根据讲话人的习惯，讲话持续时间可以从几秒（几十个字）到几分钟（几百至几千个字）不等。这种翻译方式主要用于新闻发布会、记者招待会、政治会谈、外交或商务谈判、大会发言、学术交流、开幕式和闭幕式、宴会祝酒、法庭辩论等正规场合，译员需要借助笔记进行口译；或用于迎来送往、参观陪同等日常生活中，译员通常凭记忆进行口译。

同声传译是讲话人一面讲、译员一面译的口译形式。同声传译主要用于高级别国际大型会议、经济论坛等。同声传译又具体包括三种形式，最为主要的形式为会议传译，即利用会场的同传设备进行翻译，同传设备包括同传中央控制器、红外发射主机、红外发射板、译员机、同传翻译箱、同传耳机等构成。一场国际会议需要不同语种的同传译员，每个语种的译员也不止一个，不同语种的译员使用不同的翻译箱。同传耳机将译员的声音传送给与会代表，代表们根据自己熟悉的语言选择频道收听。除了会议传译外，同传还包括视译（sight interpretation）和耳语传译（whispering）。视译指译员一面看讲稿或其他书面材料（讲话提纲、发言 PPT 等），一面翻译。这需要译员边听、边看的同时做出翻译。耳语传译指译员坐在听者旁边，把听到的话立即小声地译出来，身边人听到即可。耳语翻译可以不用一字不落全部翻译，译员一般对原讲话内容进行压缩和概括，提纲挈领的翻译。这种传译也称“咬耳朵”翻译。

与同声传译相比，交替传译因为有更多的时间思考，还可以记笔记，因此译文更加精准考究。但是在论坛口译中使用较多的为同声传译，因为与交替传译相比，同声传译更加节省时间，一般而言，交传中译员翻译占用的时间同讲话人差不多或稍多一些，由此一来，会议时间将会延长一倍，增加成本。因此在论坛的主题演讲与圆桌论坛中主要使用同声传译，在论坛的发布会和记者招待会中则使用交替传译。

2. 论坛口译原则和要求。

口译是全方位的挑战，需要译员有一定的语言功底、还要有良好的心理素质与反应能力，此外，还要具备一定的百科知识和交流技巧，同时还要注意仪态仪表。一般而言，口译要达到三个标准，即快、准、顺。“快”指的是说话者话音一落，译员就需要把话语信息传达给听众。“准”指正确地将讲话人话语内容译出，既包括说话者的观点、要点等概括性信息，也包括数字、地名、人名、职务等详细信息。“顺”指语言顺畅，无明显停顿。

论坛口译主要应用在高级别大型国际会议、论坛或研讨中，因此对译员有更高的要求，这包括语言使用准确得体流畅、语速适中，翻译忠于原话、灵活应变，无任何知识、文化方面的错误。

二、论坛口译的准备阶段

要想做好论坛口译，需要大量的前期准备，这个准备有长期的有临时的。长期准备指在语言、文化、口译技能等方面做出的几个月甚至几年的努力；临时准备指在论坛开始前的一段时间，通常为几天或几个星期，做出的搜集论坛相关的资料，获取大会发言稿，熟悉论坛相关领域语言知识点等方面的案头工作。

（一）语言知识储备

论坛口译通常包括主题发言、圆桌论坛以及新闻发布会等环节。每个部分都有一些习惯用语，需要提前掌握。

1. 论坛口译常用短语和搭配。

英译汉示例

英文	中文
Give the floor to...	请……发言。
It's great to be back at the ... Forum.	非常高兴能再次来到……论坛。
Today, I've been asked to set out the challenges and opportunities facing..., and to describe..., and I've also been asked to share some thoughts on...	今天（主办方）让我讲讲…面临的机遇和挑战，说说……，此外，再谈谈对……的想法。
I'll take these points in turn.	我将对这些要点一一进行说明。
From my point of view, that means...	依我之见，这意味着……
From my perspective as COO...	作为首席运营官，我认为……
But I will come back to where I started and say that...	但是我想再说说我最前面讲的……
Let me sum up.	我来总结一下。
So I look forward to hearing about some of your thoughts and experiences in meeting our shared challenges. Thank you.	下面我期望聆听在座的各位的想法，分享你们应对挑战的经验，谢谢。
My expectation is that next year at this conference we will be talking more about integrated solutions to some of those challenges.	我希望在明年的会议上可以更多地谈论应对这些个挑战的综合解决方法。
Join me up here today are three distinguished panelists from... industry.	今天跟我一起进行讨论的是来自……行业的三名优秀的专家。
On my far right is ... who is ..., in the middle is ... who is ..., and finally the third panelist is...	最右边的是……她/他是……，中间的是……，最后的嘉宾是……
Please give the panelists warm welcome.	请给予各位专家热烈的欢迎。

续表

英文	中文
I'd like to get the conversation started by talking about...	我们先从……谈起。
I hope each of them to speak about... and start with...	我想请在座的各位谈谈……从……开始
Thank our panelists for the very informed presentation.	谢谢专家们详细的介绍。
So let me take some questions. I'm going to start off with ... at...	下面来回答问题，先从……（媒体机构）的……（记者）开始。

汉译英示例

中文	英文
对……表示衷心的感谢	express sincere gratitude to...
以掌声对……表示的最热烈的欢迎	propose the warmest applause to...
请……讲话	Let's welcome... to give a speech
各位尊贵的领导人，各位来宾，女士们、先生们，	Distinguished leaders, dear guests, ladies and gentlemen
非常高兴能够参加第五届……高峰论坛。刚才听了一些领导专家的演讲，我觉得非常的受启发。	I'm delighted to attend the 5th ... forum. I've listened to some speeches made by leaders and experts, which inspired me a lot.
刚才……对宏观经济下的形势做了非常全面、非常深刻的分析和判断。	Just now, ... made a very comprehensive and profound analysis and judgment on the situation under macro economy.
紧迫问题	pressing issues
面临严峻挑战	face severe challenges

续表

英文	中文
以此会议为契机	take the opportunity of this seminar
预祝……取得圆满成功!	Wish ... a great success!
今天与在座的各位分享了……一些体会和心得，权当是抛砖引玉，不妥之处欢迎批评指正，谢谢大家。	Today I share with you here some thoughts and experiences on ..., simply introduce the subject for discussion. Criticism and suggestions are welcome. Thank you.
我们主题论坛请来的嘉宾就是刚刚发言的几位嘉宾。	The guests of our roundtable are those who made the speeches just now.
我们首先把话语权交给……	We first give the floor to ...
感谢五位的分享，感谢在座各位的聆听。	Thanks the guests for your sharing and thanks the audience for your kind listening.
我们不得不结束我们的主题论坛。再次让我们以热烈的掌声感谢四位的发言。	We have to end the roundtable right now. Please once again express our thanks with warm applause to four guests.
谢谢主持人给我第一个提问的机会。	Thank you for giving me this opportunity to ask the first question.
感谢各位的光临，记者招待会到此结束。	Thank you all for coming. This concludes the press conference.

2. 能源类口译短语和搭配。

英译汉示例

英文全称及简称	中文全称及简称	注释
Royal Dutch Shell plc	荷兰皇家壳牌石油公司	“plc” 为 “public limited company” 的缩写
BP	英国石油公司	前称为 “British Petroleum”（英国石油），后为 “BP”。世界最大私营石油公司之一。总部在英国伦敦。
Platts	普氏能源资讯公司	是美国麦格劳一希尔集团（The McGraw-Hill Companies，Inc.）的子公司，全球领先的能源和金属信息提供商；为石油企业提供可靠的市场价格信息，与阿格斯能源咨询公司并称石油市场最重要两家价格报告机构。
Rosneft Oil	俄罗斯石油公司	俄罗斯最大的石油公司。
Exxon Mobil	埃克森—美孚	美国一家炼油公司。
ConocoPhillips	康菲石油公司	美国一家综合性的跨国能源公司。
Saudi Aramco	沙特阿拉伯国家石油公司（阿美石油公司）	阿拉伯地区最大的石油公司之一。
Unocal	优尼科	加州联合石油公司。
Argus Media Ltd.	阿格斯能源咨询公司	英国一家独立的传媒机构，总部在伦敦，在世界各大能源中心设有办事处，主要发布能源市场的新闻、评论、价格评估、市场以及行业动向等报告。

续表

英文全称及简称	中文全称及简称	注释
Offshore Technology Conference (OTC)	国际近海技术会议	
National Oil Companies (NOCs)	国有石油企业	
upstream and downstream business	上下游业务	在石油石化行业的产业链中，上游业务指石油勘探与开发，下游业务指炼油、运输及销售等。
fossil energy	化石能源	
excessive consumption of natural resources	过度消耗自然资源	

汉译英示例

中文全称及简称	英文全称及简称
中国石油天然气集团公司（中石油）	China National Petroleum Corporation (CNPC, PetroChina)
中国石油化工集团公司（中石化）	China Petroleum & Chemical Corporation (Sinopec)
中国海洋石油总公司（中海油）	China National Offshore Oil Corporation (CNOOC)
石油巨头（大的石油公司）	oil majors/giants
海上油气资源	offshore oil and gas resources
海运石油出口量	sea borne oil exports
油田服务供应商	providers of oilfield services
页岩气	shale gas

续表

中文全称及简称	英文全称及简称
低碳经济	low carbon economy
二氧化碳排放	carbon emission reduction
可持续发展	sustainable development
开发可再生资源	develop renewable resources
提高能源利用率	too raise energy utilization efficiency
能源供需	energy supply and demand
原油产量	crude oil output
资源节约	resource conservation
油价持续上涨的压力	sustained upward pressure on oil prices
油价走高	oil prices go higher
油价保持在每桶 100 美元以上	the oil price stays above ＄100 a barrel
燃油补贴	fuel subsidies
深水油田	deep-water oilfield
深水勘探	deep-water exploration
水平钻井	horizontal drilling
上游生产	upstream production
下游市场	downstream market

上述短语及搭配仅仅是冰山一角，作为口译员要不断地积累口译词汇，还要积极关注一些新词热词，及时更新词汇库。

（二）文化常识储备

翻译除了要有很强的语言功底外，还要具备丰富的文化常识。一言以蔽之，翻译要是杂家，用英语表达，即为“Jack of all trades”（万事通）；要各行各业的情况都了解一点，但同时还要有所侧重，因此口译员通常有自己擅长翻译的领域，有的是翻译环境、能源的好手，有的则对政治、经济类翻译更加得心应手。文化常识涵盖广泛、内容丰富，任何人不可能全部掌握。作为译员，要掌握自己翻译领域中常见的知识点。

第一，对各类名称要了解，包括人名、地名、公司名、组织机构名、书籍报刊名称，等等。在2012年第四届中国石油石化产业发展国际论坛上，中国能源网首席信息官韩晓平在本次论坛发表演讲，其中提到“丹尼尔·尤金讲世界将出现一个新的石油版图，过去的石油版图以中东为中心，今天的石油版图将会以西半球。”讲话中出现了“丹尼尔·尤金”这个名字，这就考查译员的常识储备了，是否了解该人，了解他的著作，是否能够说出他的英文名字“Daniel Yergin”。他在演讲中还提到“盖特纳对中国改革的干预，他认为中国必须更多地依靠民营企业的创新，而不是国有企业的产能扩张。”这里又提到一个人名“盖特纳”，此人于2009年至2012年担任美国财政部长，英文名字为“Timothy F. Geithner”，如果译员了解此人，便可以准确度的说出他的英文名字，甚至是他的全名，还可以在翻译时，加上他的职务“US Treasury Secretary”，这无疑会使译员的译文更加专业，提高听众对译员的信赖程度。在2011年伦敦举行的“金融时报首席财务官全球能源论坛”（FT CFO Global Energy Forum）上，荷兰皇家壳牌公司首席财务官西蒙·亨利（Simon Henry）进行发言，提到：

But in recent weeks, the IEA has scaled back its oil demand growth projections.

“IEA”全称为“International Energy Agency”（国际能源署），是由经济合作发展组织（OECD）建立的国际能源机构，致力于预防石油供给的异动，并提供国际石油市场及其他能源领域的统计情报，作为译员只有提前知晓这个组织，才能将其正确的翻译。

第二，对一些基本概念的把握。在上述提到的 Simon Henry 的发言中另一句子为：

In recent days alone, we've seen a fresh warning from the US Federal Reserve about the state of the global economy.

此句中“US Federal Reserve”为“美国联邦储备系统”，简称“美联储”，负责履行美国的中央银行的职责。在第二届中国石油石化产业发展国际论坛上，中国石油和化学工业协会副会长赵俊贵在发言中提到，“我个人认为低碳经济不是一个简单的概括，也不是一个简单的碳减排，低碳经济应该是石化企业未来可持续发展的一种新的理念和一种模式”，其中包括了“碳减排”、“低碳经济”的概念，“碳减排”（carbon emission reduction）即减少二氧化碳的排放量，只有了解这个概念，口译时才不会出错；低碳经济译为“low carbon economy”。

第三，对一些常见诗句、谚语俗语的掌握。众所周知，中国国务院总理温家宝在发言时经常引经据典，作为译员要有一定的知识储备，方能做到临场不乱。在 2010 年 03 月 14 日第十一届全国人民代表大会第三次会议后的记者见面会上，温家宝总理引用屈原《离骚》里的诗句为做好之后三年的工作赋诗明志，“亦余心之所向兮，虽九死其尤未悔”，当时翻译张璐的译文为“For the ideal that I hold dear to my heart, I'd not regret a thousand times to die”，这个翻译展现了译员深厚的文化功底和临场反应能力。在大会或论坛开幕式上，为了表示欢迎，经常会引用《论语》中的名句“有朋自远方来，不亦乐乎”（Isn't it a delight to have friends coming from afar?）。对于大部分译员而言，一般都需要提前掌握一些常见诗句的译文以及诗句翻译的技巧。

（三）论坛口译技能训练

口译技能包括听、说、记忆、笔记、口译技巧等多个方面的技能。

1. 听说技能训练。

听的技能除了听力理解之外，主要练习听力记忆能力以及对于不同口音的听辨能力。提高听力记忆指提高短时记忆（short-term memory）能力。训练短期记忆需要采取循序渐进的方法。先听记词汇，然后句子，再然后段落，最后进行语篇记忆。要想提高听力记忆能力，需要练习如何快速抓住听力核心信息，即什么人、什么事、什么地方、什么时间、怎么样、为什么（who，what，where，when，how，why）。通过反复练习，逐渐扩大脑容量。

提高口译听力能力的又一突破口为熟悉不同的英语口音，尤其是说话人来自非英语母语国家，特别是中东地区、一些亚洲国家，例如印度、日本等以及一些非洲国家。练习英语口音的听力，主要是熟悉不同口音的发音规律。例如：中东地区的人讲英语受中东地区自身语言口音的影响，很多人将英语中的"R"发成"颤舌音"，听起来有点大舌头。比如他们将"喝"的英文"drink"读成"顿儿克"，将"thirty"读成"得尔提"等。日语里面包含很多外来词，很大一部分来自英语，发音也本土化了。日语从语音角度讲是以元音结尾的语言，没有辅音结尾，所以不习惯发辅音。因此经常在以辅音结尾的单词后补充一个元音，例如"领带"的英文"necktie"，日语本土发音为"nekutai"，在 k 音后加了原因 u。此外，日语中基本没有

[l] 和 [r] 音的区别，都发 [l] 音，例如："相机"的英文"camera"，日文本土发音为"kamela"。这对日本人习得英语发音造成一定的困难。印度人说英国话也有浓重的口音。由于受印地语等地方语言发音和语调的影响，印度人的英语没有爆破音和清辅音，因此把 t 和 th 读成 d、p 读成 b、k 读成 g。例如：一句话"I'd like to change the color"，会大概发音成这些字母组合的音"I'd lig do change de gala"。非洲人的英语口音与印度口音有相似的地方，即清辅音浊化：如 [t] / [k] / [p] 等，都倾向于不送气，而浊化。把 [t] 浊化成 [d]，[k] 浊化成 [g]，[p] 浊化成 [b]。另外，将"er"结尾的 [ə] 统统发成 [a]。例如，water 读成 [waːda]。掌握这些口音的发音规律，再勤加练习就可以逐步应对来自不同地区的人的英语口译了。

说的技能训练包括语音、语调、语速、句子准确性、话语流畅连贯，等等。语音方面，一些常见的发音一定要保证准确，中式英语常见的发音错误为将"Three"发成"sree"以及将"they"发成"zay"，即关于"th"咬舌音的问题。在语调语速上要注意断句，将句子在主谓宾，定状补以及各个意群的基础上娓娓道来，重点部分要重读。在句子语法准确性方面，经常比较混乱的为人称代词"ta（他、她、它）"的翻译，在进行汉英口译时，听到"ta"的音，可以译成"he"，"she"或"it"，要快速做出正确选择，一旦出错，会造成观众极大的困扰。另外，单复数也是汉英口译容易出错的地方，因为汉语中名词没有复数形式，因此英译时经常使用名词的单数形式，造成语法错误。例如："近几年相继落成的钻井平台"很容易在口译中译成"the drilling platform having completed in the past few years"，实际上"钻井平台"应使用复数形式

"platforms"。

2. 口译笔记能力训练。

在正式会议或国际论坛的交替传译中，为了保证译文的全面和准确，口译员在听的时候会做笔头记录，随后根据笔记内容进行翻译。

(1) 口译笔记的构成

1) 字母

为了达到快速记录的目的，在口译笔记中几乎无法记录完整单词，因此会使用一些字母、缩写和符号来代替单词或短语。此外，笔记还使用一些线条和箭头表示指代关系。

常见字母缩写

字母	所指	意义
e	economy，economic	经济
E	energy	能源
f	finance，financial	金融
h	hour	小时
j	project	工程，项目
m	minute	分钟
M	month	月
p	politics	政治
	political	政治的
	party	政党
	policy	政策
Q	say，speak，talk	说
R	research	研究

续表

字母	所指	意义
s	science	科学
	society	社会
t	time	时间
V	victory，win	胜利
w	week	周

常见字母组合缩写

字母组合	所指	意义
ad	advertisement	广告
adm	administration	管理
app	apply，application	应用
co	company	公司
ctrl	control	控制
demo	demonstration	展示
doc	document	文档
edu	education	教育
fm	form	形式
	foam	泡沫
info	information	信息
memo	memorandum	备忘录，纪要
msg	message	信息
std	standard	标准
str	street	街道
tel	telephone	电话
thx	thanks	谢谢

常见国家或城市缩写

国家或城市缩写	所指	意义
Afg	Afghanistan	阿富汗
Bra	Brazil	巴西
Ca	Canada	加拿大
Fr	France	法国
Ind	India	印度
Ir	Iran	伊朗
Ita	Italy	意大利
Qat	Qatar	卡塔尔
Rus	Russia	俄罗斯
SA	Saudi Arabia	沙特阿拉伯
UK	United Kingdom	英国
US	United States	美国
BJ	Beijing	北京
SH	Shanghai	上海
LA	Los Angeles	洛杉矶
NY	New York	纽约

常见机构缩写

机构缩写	所指	意义
APEC	Asia-Pacific Economic Cooperation	亚太经济合作组织
ASEAN	Association of Southeast Asian Nations	东南亚国家联盟
BRICs	Brazil，Russia，India，China	金砖四国（巴西、俄罗斯、印度和中国）
BFA	Boao Forum for Asia	博鳌亚洲论坛
EU	European Union	欧盟
GATT	General Agreement on Tariffs and Trade	关税及贸易总协定
ICC	International Chamber of Commerce	国际商会
IEA	International Energy Agency	国际能源署
IMO	International Maritime Organization	国际海事组织
IOC	International Olympic Committee	国际奥林匹克委员会
NASA	National Aeronautics and Space Administration	美国国家航空和宇宙航行局
OPEC	Organization of Petroleum Exporting Countries	石油输出国组织
OECD	Organization for Economic Co-operation and Development	经济合作与发展组织
UN	United Nations	联合国
UNDP	United Nations Development Programme	联合国开发计划署
UNEP	United Nations Environment Programme	联合国环境署
UNESCO	United Nations Educational，Scientific，and Cultural Organization	联合国教科文组织
WEC	World Energy Council	世界能源理事会
WTO	World Trade Organizaiton	国际贸易组织

其他缩略语缩写

缩略语	所指	意义
BBC	British Broadcasting Corporation	英国广播公司
CNN	Cable News Network	美国有线电视新闻网络
AP	Associated Press	美国联合通讯社
NHK	Nippon Hoso Kyokai	日本广播协会
PM	Prime Minister	首相，总理
CEO	Chief Executive Officer	首席执行官；执行总裁
CFO	Chief Finance Officer	首席财务官
COO	Chief Operating Officer	首席运营官
M&A	Mergers and Acquisitions	企业并购

2）常见符号

符号示例

符号	所指	意义
$\overline{\mathrm{d}}$	morning	上午
$\underline{\mathrm{d}}$	afternoon	下午
$\overline{\mathrm{M}}$	the first ten-day of a month	一个月的上旬
~~M~~	the second ten-day of a month	一个月的中旬
$\underline{\mathrm{M}}$	the third ten-day of a month	一个月的下旬
· d	yesterday	昨天
y ·	next year	明年
+	more，add	更多
—	minus，except	除了
∵	because，due to	因为
∴	so，therefore	所以

续表

符号	所指	意义
×	wrong, bad	错误，不好
√	correct, good	正确，好的
>	more than	比……多
<	less than	比……少
=	the same, equal	相同，相等
≠	different	不同
≈	about, nearly, similar	大约，类似
[ ]	within, during	在……期间，在……当中
:	express, show	表达，表明
?	problem, question	问题
!	dangerous, careful	危险，仔细
~	last (vt.)	持续
_	this, here	这个，此
…	many	很多
/		用于分隔意群
)		将几项并列的内容括在一起
□	state, nation, country	国家
⊡	domestic, internal, home	国内
□•	foreign, oversea, abroad	国外
□→	export, go abroad	出口
→□	import, come to the country	进口
☆	important, outstanding	重要
><	conflict, clash	矛盾，冲突
⊥	disagreement	分歧

续表

符号	所指	意义
∽	exchange，relations	关系，交换
*	feature，typical	特点，典型
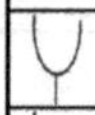	agreement，contract	协议，合同
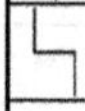	preside，host	主持
≡	maintain，stable	维持，稳定
	eye，look at，witness	看，目击
	delete，solve，get rid of	清除，去除
<	open	开放
○	whole，empty	全部
	develop，development	发展
	fruit，consequence，achievement	果实，结果
⊙	meeting，meet	会议，会面
◎	environment	环境
○文	school，college	学校
△	aim，target	目标，目的
°	people	人
ˆ	top，head，lead	带领，头

3）线条和箭头

线条和箭头示例

线条和箭头	所指	意义
	in the past	过去
	in future，in the future	未来
↑	increase，grow，up	增长

续表

线条和箭头	所指	意义
↓	decrease，fall，down	下降
←	invited，come	邀请，来到
→	go to	前往，去
	return，come back	返回
		表示笔记内容有逻辑关联

4）其他

其他方式示例

其他方式	所指	意义
力	powerful，strong	力量，强壮
饣	food	食物
GX	relations，relationship	关系
RX	honor，privilege	荣幸
xie	thank you	谢谢
¥	RMB，interest	人民币，利益
$	dollar，money	美元，钱
€	euro	欧元
æ	act，implement，do	行为，做

（2）口译笔记方法

做口译笔记即如何使用上述各种缩写和符号记录信息。对于口译笔记有两个要求：第一，记录全面，第二，容易识别。要满足这两个要求，笔记一定要有逻辑，信息记录不是符号的简单堆砌，要重点突出。口译笔记在记什么怎么记上面有几点原则：第一，记录重点信息，包括：数字（年代、日期、产量，等等）、各类名称（人名、地名、组织，等等）、表明意义的各类实词（名词、动词、部分形容词和副词）；第二，表示时态、语态、复数等语法词或字母一般不予记录。第三，对于使用哪种语言、哪个符号记录没有任何规定，全凭译员自己的意愿。第四，记录信息横向不要太长，要尽量从上向下采用倒梯形记录。具体笔记方法见下例所示。

讲话原文	口译笔记
Located in the region of Pengerang, Johor, Malaysia, Project RAPID is a substantial oil refining and petrochemical integrated engineering project owned by PETRONAS.	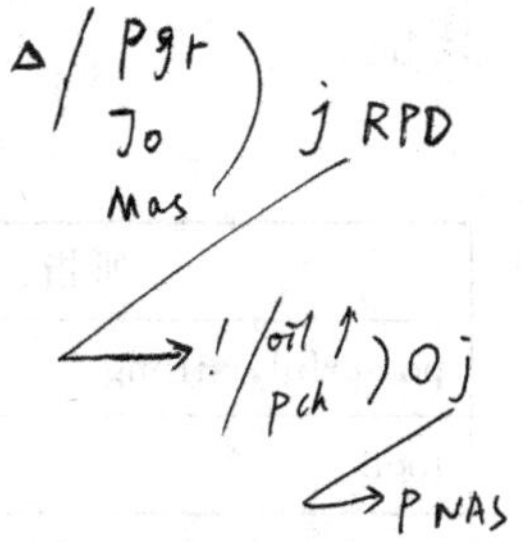
The whole upstream cycle can last half a century or more. Samotlor marks its 50th anniversary next year for example. And the first seismic was shot in the North Sea 50 years ago this year.	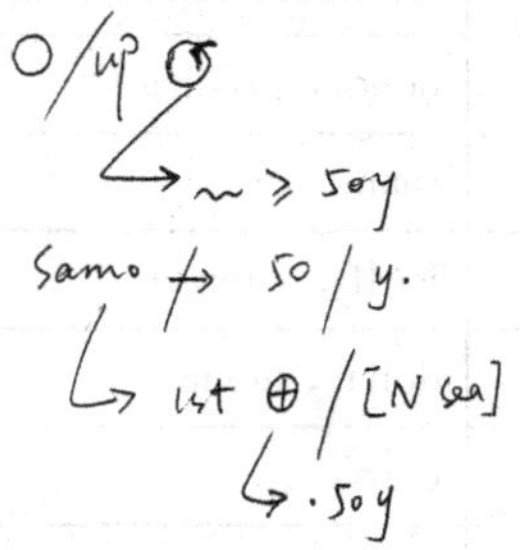
2014年上半年，世界经济增速回落，中国经济保持增长，成品油需求增速放缓，化工产品价格下滑，但本公司仍实现经营收益双位数增长。	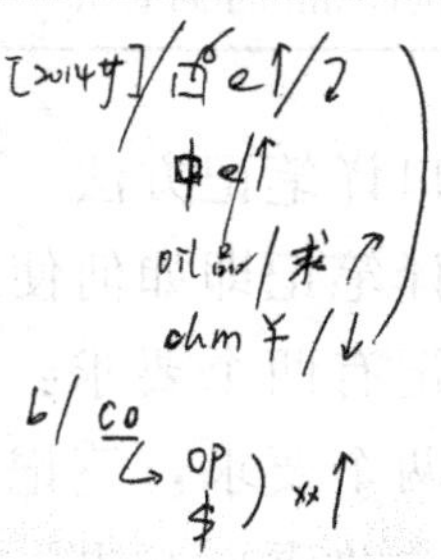

续表

讲话原文	口译笔记
根据合同，中国联合石油有限责任公司自合同签订之日起三年内，每天将从委内瑞拉购买 10 万桶燃料油。至此，中国石油 2014 年对委内瑞拉油品贸易量将达到 79 万桶/日，成为委内瑞拉最大的油品贸易商之一。	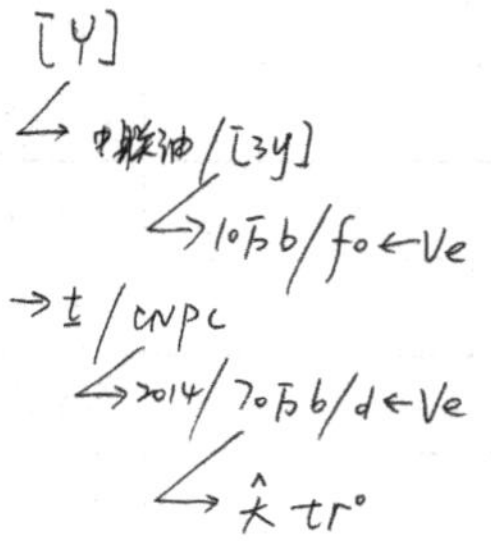

根据上述例子可以概括出他们的共同特点：

1）笔记使用了大量的缩写、符号和箭头。

上表第一栏中的缩写和符号

缩写和符号	所指	译文
Pgr	Pengerang	边佳兰
Jo	Johor	柔佛
Mas	Malaysia	马来西亚
j	project	工程
RPD	RAPID	工程的名称
p ch	petrochemical	石化的
P NAS	PETRONAS	马来西亚石油
△	located in	地点，位于
○	integrated	综合的

上表第二栏中的缩写和符号

缩写和符号	所指	译文
up	upstream	上游
50y	half a century	半个世纪
Samo	Samotlor	萨莫特洛尔油田
1st	first	首个，第一个
N	North	北
○	whole	全部的
↻	cycle	周期
⊕	shot	开始
y·	next year	明年
·50y	50 years ago	50 年前

上表第三栏中的缩写和符号

缩写和符号	所指	译文
e	economy	经济
中	中国	China
oil 品	成品油	refined oil products
求	需求	demand
chm	化工产品	chemicals
b	但	but
Co	本公司	this company
	上半年	the first half of the year
	世界	world
↑	增长	increase
↗	缓慢增长	slow growth

续表

缩写和符号	所指	译文
¥	价格	price
↓	下滑	drop
$	收益	profit
××↑	双位数增长	double digit increase

上表第四栏中的缩写和符号

缩写和符号	所指	译文
中联油	中国联合石油	China National United Oil Coporation
3y	三年	three years
b	barrel	桶
f o	fuel oil	燃油
Ve	委内瑞拉	Venezuela
CNPC	中国石油	
t	此时	by this time, at the moment
d	天	day
Y.	合同	contract
←	从……购买	buy from
→	至，到	till
^大	最大的	the biggest
tr°→	贸易商	trader, business partner

上述缩写和符号的使用并不唯一，译员可以根据自己的习惯选用适合自己的。例如："Malaysia"的缩写除了上述"Mas"外，还可以缩写为"MY"；"中国"的缩写除了汉字"中"外，还可以缩写成"CN"。箭头的使用比较频繁，要注

意区别，表示“增长”使用向上的箭头“↑”，如果表示“缓慢增长”则使用斜向上的箭头“↗”；左箭头“←”表示“来到”，右箭头“→”表示“前往”。此外，还有一些缩写和符号的组合，例如“y·”表示明年，圆点在表示“年”的缩写“y”右边表示“下一年”，而圆点在“y”的左边表示“以前的”，因此“·50y”表示“50 年前”；“tr°”是缩写“tr”和右上角小圆圈的组合，“tr”是“trade”（贸易）的缩写，圆圈表示“人”，组合在一起表示“贸易商”。

2）笔记中使用分隔符“/”来隔开句子的各个成分或意群。并且每行的意群不超过 3 个。这种记录方法是笔记结构更加清晰，更有逻辑性。

3）用斜向下向右的箭头“↘”表示下文对上文的接续，增添笔记的完整性。

4）并列的成分一行一个内容，并用大括号将并列的成分括起来，如例 1 中的所示。

综上所述，口译笔记有一定的规律可循，例如记录采用短行并且一直向下延伸的方法，但是也有强烈的个人特色，每个译员原则使用的笔记符号会有所不同，记录的内容也不尽相同。无论如何，口译笔记是广泛应用在交替传译当中的非常重要的口译技能。

3. 口译技巧训练。

（1）顺句驱动（linear interpretation）

顺句驱动，即顺译法。“顺译”并不意味着完全字对字、词对词的翻译，而是指尽可能按照句中概念或意群出现的先后顺序将原语整体意思译出。英汉两种语言在语序和词序上有很大差异，但是不可否认两种语言存在着很多共性，例如：主谓宾的句子结构，喝水、刷牙的动宾搭配，等等。这使得顺句驱动的翻译方法成为可能。顺译可以减少记忆的压力，从而减轻认知负荷，顺句驱动在及时存储信息和适时调整词序上最为省时省力，是同声传译最有效的策略，见下例所示。

例 1：

现场还有很多媒体朋友，他们对本次会议的成功召开给予了很大的帮助，对此我谨致以诚挚的谢意。

顺译：Here today come a lot of media friends. They help a lot for the successful commencement of this conference, so I wish to express our sincere thanks to them.

例 2：

I' ve described the steps taken by Shell ' s finance function to create value in our major projects.

顺译：我已经说明了壳牌公司财务部门采取的一些措施，这些措施为我们的重大项目创造了价值。

在例 1 中，如果是笔译，为了句子的逻辑和完整，最好译成“I wish to express my thanks to the media friends here today who help a lot for the successful commencement of this conference.”但是在同传口译中，一般要求译员要在讲话人开始讲话后几秒钟或者半句话后开始翻译，因此只能听到哪儿翻到哪儿，根据原句顺序将感谢的对象先翻译，然后再表达感谢。例 2 的英文原文包括了“过去分词做定语”以及“不定式”，句子结构复杂。要想按照顺句驱动的方法翻译，需要及时断句。因此先翻译前半句“I’ve described the steps taken by Shell’s finance function”，然后翻译“to create value in our major projects.”为了前后连贯，为后半句加上主语“steps”。由此可见，使用顺译法要准确的断句，要前后兼顾，在必要时进行一定的补充说明。

（2）重复法

重复法也是口译员频频使用的技巧。上述例 2 中，在两句译文衔接时“这些措施”便是重复了前半句的词汇。重复除了可以使语言保持连贯，让表达更加清楚易懂外，还可以增加思考的时间，见下例所示。

例 1：

We have advocated the principle of mutual benefit and common development, which is now growing more and more popular in international trade.

译文：我们提倡互惠互利、和平共处的原则，这项原则目前在世界上已越来越得人心了。

例 2：

我们致力于提高产品的质量和数量，同时要多开发分销渠道。

We are committed to improve both the quality and quantity of our product, and we also at the same time try to develop distribution channel.

例 1 中，口译时将定语从句指示词 which 具体指代的内容译出，重复前文“原则”一词；例 2 中在翻译并列成分的时候，为了加深听众印象，将主语 we 重复了。由此可见，英汉互译中重复无处不在，尤其是在翻译英语定语从句的时候以及汉语短句的时候。

除了顺译和重复，口译中还可以应用“增译”、“省译”、“拆分”、词性转化等技巧。很多技巧与笔译的相同，在此不一一赘述。

（四）论坛资料准备

再好的口译员在担任论坛口译前也需要大量收集论坛相关资料，做好充分准备。一般包括论坛的主题、日程、参加的主要领导、领导的职位、主持词，等等。

1. 论坛历史和主题。

参加论坛前，要对该论坛具备最基本的了解，包括论坛中英文名称，什么时候建立，参与人情况，历届论坛举办地，历届论坛主题，等等。这些有助于译员预测论坛的主旨与研讨主题，可以提前做好准备。

2. 主题发言人及发言大纲。

如果可以，译员要提前向论坛主办方询问主持人以及发言人的情况，并索要主持词和发言稿或发言大纲。了解发言人情况可以知晓他/她的英语发音情况，英语是否为其母语，是否有特别的口音，以便提前进行口音适应练习。一般而言，论坛主办方会在论坛前三天将发言人的发言稿交到译员手中，不过有时译员需要主动索要，方可获得。在了解了论坛主题和发言内容后，便可搜集材料，做好专业知识，语言知识方面的准备了。

三、论坛口译的实施阶段

大型国际论坛一般持续几天，每天的活动内容不同，包括开幕式和领导致辞、主题发言、分组讨论、圆桌会谈等，基本使用同声传译。有时候还有一个对外的新闻发布会，如果需要翻译则多使用交替传译。小型论坛一般只举办一两天，如果参加人基本使用两种语言，例如中文和英文，则大部分使用交替传译。另外，会场是否设有同传设备是会议是否使用同声传译的根本决定因素。

（一）论坛同声传译

同声传译为论坛的基本翻译形式，通常由两个译员交替完成，每个译员持续工作半个小时左右。当一个译员翻译时，另一个译员做一些提示、辅助的工作，包括题词、监控等，当然另一个译员也可以利用等待的时间稍作休息。同声传译是即时翻译，基本不需要译员做笔记，这要求译员有较强的记忆能力以及快速的反应能力，还要有丰富的知识储备以及预测能力。

下文的开幕式致辞节选于第四届“国际能源论坛暨国际气体联合会”部长级气体论坛（4th IEF-IGU Ministerial Gas Forum），举办时间为2014年11月12日，地点为墨西哥的阿卡普尔科。致辞人为国际能源论坛（International Energy Forum）秘书长（Secretary General）奥尔多·弗洛里斯·基罗加（Aldo Flores-Quiroga），译文为笔者自译，仅供参考。

节选一	
His Excellency, Pedro Joaquín Coldwell, Secretary of Energy of Mexico, Mr. Jerome Ferrier, President of the International Gas UnionMr. Luis Vázquez, President of the Mexican Natural Gas Association Excellencies Ladies and Gentlemen,	尊敬的墨西哥能源部长佩德罗·华金·科德韦尔阁下，尊敬的国际气体联合会主席杰罗姆·费列尔阁下，尊敬的墨西哥天然气联合会主席路易斯·瓦兹库兹阁下，女士们、先生们，
节选二	
Good morning and welcome to the 4th IEF-IGU Ministerial Gas Forum! It is great to have you here in Mexico—my home country. Let me thank the government of Mexico for its great hospitality-and especially Minister Pedro Joaquín Coldwell, for his leadership and support to the global energy dialogue; and for taking the initiative of hosting this conversation among Ministers and CEOs.	大家上午好，欢迎来到第四届“国际能源论坛暨国际气体联合会”部长级气体论坛。非常高兴大家来到墨西哥，我的祖国。 首先我要感谢墨西哥政府的热情接待，尤其感谢佩德罗·华金·科德韦尔部长，正是他的领导和支持成就了本次全球能源对话，感谢他主动主办本次部长以及企业领导人之间的对话。
节选三	
I think you will agree with me that we are at an ideal place to talk about “The Role of Gas in Energy Security and Sustainable Economic Development”, the theme of this Ministerial meeting. As you are aware, this summer the president of Mexico — Enrique Peña Nieto — signed into law an energy reform that opens the Mexican energy sector to private participation for the first time in seventy years. Mexico's gas industry will be stronger as a consequence. We will be hearing this afternoon about this reform—and I encourage you to take it as a case study and exchange points of view on its implications for national and international energy policies and strategies.	我相信在座的各位都会对此表示认同，我们所在的墨西哥是探讨“气体在能源安全以及经济可持续发展中的角色”理想的地方，这也是本次部长级会议的主题。大家都了解到，今年夏天墨西哥总统恩里克·培尼亚·涅托签署了能源改革法，将墨西哥能源领域向私营企业开放，这是70年来的第一次。墨西哥气体工业实力会变得更加强大。今天下午我们会听到此项改革的内容，借此我想鼓励大家将墨西哥能源改革作为一个案例进行讨论，探讨它对国家以及国际能源政策和策略有何启示。

续表

节选四	
Much is happening, then, in gas markets that merits discussion. How they evolve will influence the course of global energy security and the environment. That is why this IEF, IGU Ministerial Forum exists, and I trust your dialogue today contributes to your understanding of the potential and risks involved in gas policy and investment.	气体市场有很多事件是值得讨论的。这一市场的发展状况将会影响全球能源安全与环境的进程。这也是我们为什么召开此次论坛的目的。我相信今天你们之间的对话将会有助于你们了解气体政策和气体投资的潜力和风险。
节选五	
Before I give the microphone to Jérôme Ferrier, my colleague and friend who presides over the IGU, our partner in this Forum, let me underscore that, whatever your perspective, whatever your approach to policy, it will be incomplete without good data to assess the supply and demand balance. Policymakers and investors rely on it. Orderly markets require it.	在我将话筒给热罗姆·费列尔之前，我还有一些话要说。我的一些负责国际气体联合会的同事和朋友以及我们的论坛合作伙伴让我要着重强调无论你们的观点是什么，无论你们如何制定政策，如果没有有效的数据来评估供需平衡，这样的政策是不完整的。政策制定者以及投资者们都需要这样的数据，有序的市场也离不开这些数据。
节选六	
Welcome once again to Mexico and to the 4th IEF—IGU Ministerial Gas Forum! May this meeting be all you want it to be. Thank you.	再一次欢迎大家来到墨西哥参加第四届“国际能源论坛暨国际气体联合会”部长级气体论坛。希望本次论坛如大家所愿，能够取得成功。谢谢。

上文为开幕式致辞的节选，包括介绍参与论坛的主要领导、表示欢迎、表明论坛主题、论坛召开的目的，以及号召参加人加强讨论，等等。由于是同传，基本采用顺序驱动的翻译

方法，语序调整只在句子的局部进行。现将一些有代表性的译文进行说明。节选一主要是对领导的介绍，关键是人名及职务的翻译，如果没提前做好准备，这对任何译员都是极具挑战性的。如果论坛开始前已经拿到这些人名单，则会做到游刃有余。“Excellency”译为“阁下”，增译了“尊敬的”，并且翻译时将职务放在人名前，这使得译文更符合汉语的表达习惯。节选二的第一小段完全按照英文语序进行翻译，第一句由“and”连接两个短句，“good morning”和“welcome to the…Forum”，翻译时即时断句，“and”千万不要译出，当成两个句子处理。节选二的第二段使用了重复法，“Let me thank the government of Mexico for … and especially Minister Pedro Joaquín Coldwell，for …；and for…”，英文中只提到一次“thank”，但是感谢的内容却有三个，分别用“for”提出来，译成中文时，使用了三个“感谢”，见上文译文。重复不仅表现了发言人的诚意，还使汉语译文的结构更加严谨。节选三的第一个大长句用了断句的方法，尤其将“agree with me”与后面“that”引导的宾语从句断开，使译文不宜过长，这时需要增译“agree with”的宾语，可以译为“同意这一说法”或是“对此表示同意”等。另外一处明显断句的地方为把“signed into law an energy reform”与“ that opens the Mexican energy sector”断开。该句为定语从句，“reform”作前半句的宾语后半句的主语，如果翻成一句话，按照中文习惯，定语要提前，译文为“签署开放墨西哥能源领域的能源改革法”，在口译中这无疑增加译员以及听众的认知负荷，因此断开，各自成句，译为“签署能源改革法，（法律规定）将开放墨西哥的能源领域”。在节选四中，翻译时将“contributes to your understanding of the potential and risks involved in gas policy and investment”的语序做了调整，当顺序驱动实在无法进行时，只能局部调整语序。在“of”的所有格中，必须先翻译“of”后的内容，即译成“有助于你们对潜力和风险进行了解”，如果采用词性转化的技巧，可以把“understanding”译成动词，则可以仍然按照语序译为“有助于了解潜力和风险”，然而这样翻仍然不完整，听众会问“哪方面的潜力和风险”，于是后面的过去分词定语最好提前，译为“气体政策和投资上的潜力和风险”。如果译员按照顺句驱动已经译到了“potential and risks”，没有预测到后面还有定语“involved in gas policy and investment”，这时需要使用重复以及增译法，使后面的句子变得完整，可以译为“有助于了解潜力和风险，这些潜力和风险是在气体政策和投资时需要考虑的”，这个译文没有调整语序后的译文精简，但是观众也能接受。节选五中“it will be incomplete without good data to assess”这句话也需要调整语序，将条件状语“without good data to assess”先翻，“如果没有有效的数据评估…这样的政策就不完整”，同时译文中将“it”指代的内容翻出来了，为“政策”。节选六的祝福语“May this meeting be all you want it to be.”是典型的英文表达，如果直译为“希望本次论坛是你想要的论坛”，则不符合中文的表达习惯，因此根据发言人的用意，将此句译为“希望本次论坛如大家所愿，能够取得成功”。

下文的主题发言节选自第四届中国石油石化产业发展国际论坛，该论坛于2012年6月28至29日在北京举行，发言人为中国石油和化学工业联合会常务副会长李寿生，所列译文为笔者自译，仅供参考。

节选	译文
刚才侯云春主任对宏观经济下行形势做了非常全面、非常深刻的分析和判断，特别提出来要理性看待经济下行，要淡定应对形势变化，他在宏观经济形势分析之后，结合我们石油石化行业的特点，对我们如何加快结构调整提出了建议，我的发言在侯主任发言基础上，结合行业的特点，做一点发言。我的发言题目是从石油化工大国向强国跨越的战略选择。	Just now, Director Hou Yunchun made a speech on macro economy downturn situation, very comprehensive, and of incisive analysis and judgment. He particularly pointed out we should view the economic downturn on a rational perspective, and we should keep calm in coping with the situation changes. By considering the features of the petroleum and petrochemical industry, on how to accelerate structure adjustment, I'd like to make some suggestions. Based on Director Hou's speech and taking the features of this industry into account, my speech is entitled "the strategic choice of converting from petroleum and petrochemical big country to strong country" .
谈到我们行业发展战略的时候，我们都不会忘记，特别我们石油石化行业的人员都不会忘记2010年，2010年是十一五结束时期，通过十一五计划的奋斗，建国以来六十年的奋斗，我们石油石化在2010年站在了一个新的发展起点上。2010年我们国家石油石化总产值达到8.76万亿人民币，成为当今世界上仅次于美国的第二个石油化工大国，其中我们化学工业总产值达到5.14万亿，化学工业总产值超过了美国，跃居世界第一。	Speaking of the development strategy of this industry, we barely forget, especially for those who are in the petroleum and petrochemical industry, the year of 2010. This year marks the end of the 11th "five-year plan" . After these five years hardworking or the 60 years hardworking since the establishment of new China, the petroleum and petrochemical industry in the year of 2010 stood on a new starting line of development. In 2010, China's petroleum and petrochemical output reached 8.76 trillion RMB, ranking only second to US. The petrochemical output accounted for 5.14 trillion RMB, surpassing US in rank and became world No. 1.

续表

节选	译文
我最近看了看美国几大石油公司和我们中石油、中石化、中还有的差距，一个很大的差距，我们石油公司是大的，美国公司是专业化的石油公司，加快我们国家生产性服务业的发展，是我们十二五发展的一个重要的方面。这是我们国家高端发展、创新发展、绿色发展、差异化发展的几个重要内容，我们现在是石油化工大国，但不是石油化工强国，什么叫石油化工强国呢？我认为石油化工强国至少有四个标准。…这四个标志和我们石油化工发展现状来讲还有不小的距离，所以石油化工工业如何实现由大国向强国的转变，十二五期间我们任务非常艰巨。我今天就给大家介绍这么多，讲的不对的地方请大家批评指正。谢谢大家！	Recently I've noticed the differences between the major oil companies in US and those in China, including PetroChina and Sinopec. Ours are big, while those in US are specialized ones. Therefore, accelerating the development of China's productive service industry is an essential aspect of the 12th "five-year plan", and also very important to realize China's high-end development, innovative development, green development and differentiated development. China is now a petroleum and petrochemical big country, not a strong country. What would a strong one look like? In my opinion, there are at least four standards—these four standards is still beyond the reach of China's present petroleum and petrochemical industry. So how to achieve the conversion from a big country to a strong one is a very arduous task for us during the 12th "five-year plan". That's all for my speech today. If anything inappropriate, criticism and correction are welcome. Thank you!

上文为主题发言的节选，发言人先回顾了前一个发言人的主题，引出自己的发言主题，然后开始论述。汉语是意会的语言，注重意思的表达，而在语法和句子结构上比较松散。因此翻译时，除了词汇搭配外，找到合适的英文句型也是翻译的要点。在节选一中，使用了增词法、省译法、句子拆分与合并法。在口译中，译员是看不到标点的，只能根据意思自己句读。这时在一个意思表达清楚后，要完结句子。因此当听到"刚才侯云春主任对宏观经济下行形势做了非常全面、非常深

刻的分析和判断，”就可以当成一个完整句子翻译。接下来的短句“特别提出来要理性看待经济下行，要淡定应对形势变化，”当成另一个完整句子看待。在第二句翻译时，补上主语“He”，译为“He particularly pointed out…”。由此可见，面对汉语中一个又一个短句，要在联系较松散的短句间拆开分别译成完整句，而把联系紧密的短句合并译成一个长句。再看句子“我的发言在侯主任发言基础上，结合行业的特点，做一点发言。”，其中包含重复的成分，在翻译时进行省译，译为“My speech is based on Director Hou's speech and takes the features of the industry into account.”后面的“做一点发言”去掉不译。节选二的翻译重点是数字以及一些专有名词。数字口译是口译的重点，同时也是难点。由于英汉有些数字之间不能很好地找到对应的词汇，增加了数字翻译的难度。例如对于中文“三百”的翻译并不难，因为英文中有相对应的词“hundred”，而对于“三亿”的翻译就不容易了，因为英文中没有相应的词汇，要转译成“three hundred million”（三百个百万）或“point 3 billion”（零点三个十亿）。节选二中提到的单位“万亿”有直接对应的英文“trillion”，因此翻译起来并不难。此外，本节选中包含了“十一五计划”，节选三中提到了“十二五”，这是中国的经济发展规划，五年为一个阶段，有固定的译法，为“the 11th five-year plan”，“the 12 five-year plan”。节选三中，“看了看”不能直译成“look at”，“see”等词，发言人想表达的意思为“发现”或“注意到”，因此译为“find”或“notice”更合适。节选三中使用的另外一个口译技巧为预测。有人形容做口译就好像由他人领着走路，自己也不知道路到底通向何方，但随着口译经验的积累，还是可以做出一定预测的。例如节选三中的句子“加快我们国家生产性服务业的发展，是我们十二五发展的一个重要的方面。”可以作为一个完整句翻译，然而后面的句子是“这是我们国家高端发展…”，有经验的译员可以大胆预测，后面的核心词仍然是“重要方面”，往后继续听，会发现是“重要内容”，因此可以等句子还没有完全出来的时候，就使用“（it is）important to realize China's high-end development”的句子结构。

综上所述，在同声传译中，译员主要按照顺句驱动的方法进行翻译，在翻译中为了使句子更加通顺，并且符号目标语的表达习惯，会使用很多翻译技巧，例如断句，拆句、合并、增译、省译、词性转化、词义选择，等等。

（二）论坛交替传译

论坛有时候会使用交替传译，这需要译员边听边记笔记，然后用话筒将译文说出，译员一般坐在发言人的旁边，听众是能看到译员的，这为译员工作增加了一定的负担。但是成熟的译员，要适应各种情况，直面各种压力。与同传相比，交传有记笔记和思考的时间，因此译文的句子结构可以更复杂一些，用词更讲究一些。交替传译需要译员有非常强的大脑记忆能力以及手写速记能力。

下文的口译原文节选自荷兰皇家壳牌美国公司总裁马文·奥德姆（Marvin Odum）于 2012 年 11 月 29 日在纽约举行的普氏全球能源展望论坛（Platts Global Energy Outlook Forum）上的主题发言，题为“Future of Energy: Solutions Through Cooperation”（能源的未来——协同合作共谋对策）。口译笔记与译文均为笔者所写所译，仅供参考。

节选内容	口译笔记	译文
If I was going to play the "how the world is changing" card today I would go on to talk about the revolution in natural gas.	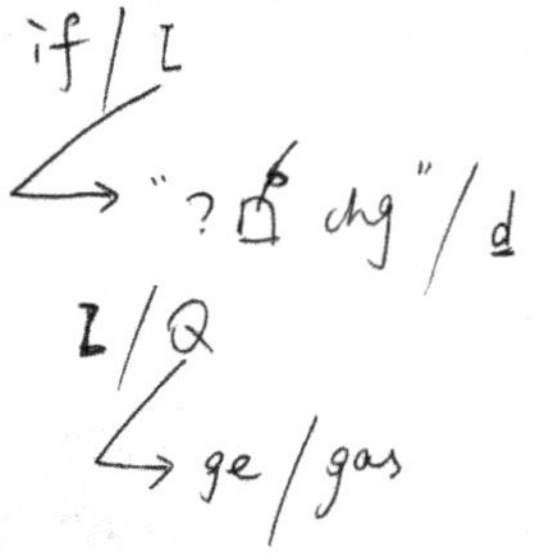	如果今天讨论的话题是"世界正在如何改变"，我想谈谈天然气革命。
That revolution is real. America suddenly has a 100 year supply of natural gas "in the bank" and the world has 250 years — thanks in part to breakthroughs in the technology that unlock hydrocarbons from tight rock and shale.	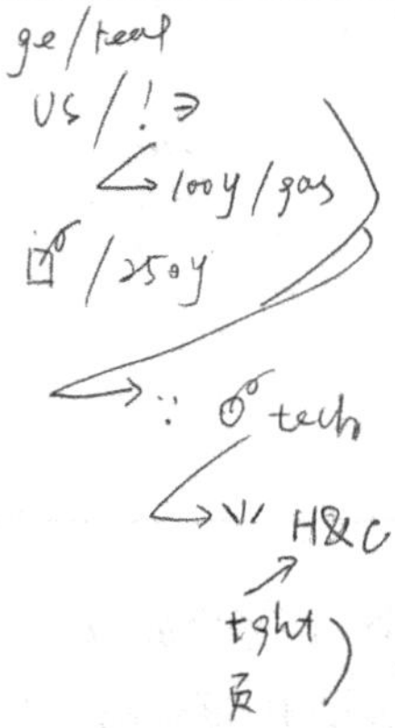	天然气革命是现实。美国突然拥有了足够使用 100 年的天然气储量，全世界的储量可以使用 250 年。在某种程度上要感谢技术突破，能够从致密岩以及页岩中释放碳氢化合物。
These new resources are not just a source of energy but a source of cleaner, more affordable, more secure energy than any other of a similar scale.	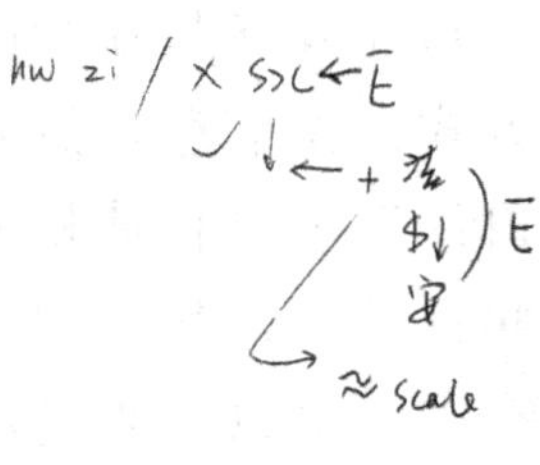	这些新资源不仅仅是一种能量的来源，与类似规模的其他能源相比，他们更洁净、更实惠，更安全。

续表

节选内容	口译笔记	译文
Shell is already the world's leader in Liquefied Natural Gas (LNG). Shell ventures delivered more than thirty percent of all the world's LNG volumes in 2011. We have eight LNG projects in operation today with three new projects under construction globally, served by 52 LNG tankers and delivering clean — burning energy to markets around the world.	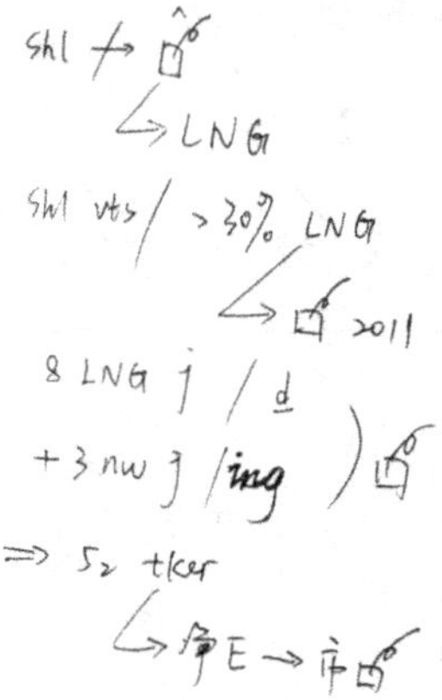	壳牌已经是世界液化天然气的领先企业。壳牌的合资企业在2011年生产的液化天然气占世界总量的30%以上。现在全球范围内我们有8个液化天然气工程已经上马，3个在建。共计52艘油轮将液化天然气这种清洁能源运往全球市场。

上文分别列出了每个节选的原文、速记笔记和译文。交替传译没有紧跟发言人的话语传译，而是等发言人结束一部分讲话停顿时，开始翻译。这需要译员在听的时候充分调动大脑记忆以及笔头记录两种方式保留信息，然后根据这些记录进行翻译。因此大脑记忆与口译笔记是相辅相成的，对于记忆力好的译员，笔记就简单一些；反之，如果记忆力偏弱，则笔记要全面一些。在口译笔记一中，可以很明显看出包含两部分，分别以If开头与I开头，体现了笔记的逻辑性，因此笔记需要记录一些表示逻辑关系的词，例如：but，additionally，thus，等等。另外，字母Q表示“talk about”，这个用法来源于QQ——一个中国使用最为广泛的聊天工具；汉语拼音ge表示“revolution”（革命），这样记录是因为无论是英文缩写“revol“或“rvlt”还是汉字“革”都没有拼音书写起来简单。在看

着笔记翻译的时候，“”会是一个挑战，此时需要调动大脑记忆，回想起“?”指代的是“how”，而不是“what”，“why”等疑问词。口译笔记二使用了曲线箭头、大括号来表示每一行笔记之间的关系。第一行“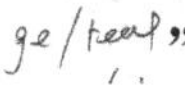”独立成句。下面的笔记用一个又一个曲线箭头连接，在讲述同一项内容，即“gas ‘in the bank’”（石油储备）。数学符号“∵”表示造成这么多天然气储备的原因，“+”表示比较级。符号“”表示“breakthrough”（突破）。节选三包括一个英文句型“not ... but ...”（不是……而是……），在笔记中体现为“”。另外，笔记中用拼音“zi”表示“resources”（资源），字母加音标的缩写“s□c”表示“source”（来源），汉字“洁”表示“clean”（洁净），“安”表示“secure”（安全）。在英汉口译中有时候用汉语拼音或汉字记录，表示译员已经一边记录一边翻译了，哪个缩写或符号最先出现在脑海里，就使用哪个。从换行、曲线箭头以及大括号可以看出口译笔记四包含了四个内容。一般一个新的内容开始都要顶头记录，未完成的换行缩进。数学符号“+”表示“另外还有”，字母组合“ing”表示“正在进行中的事务”。“⇒”表示上面的内容导致了下面的内容的发生，可以表示“这样一来”，“促使”，等含义。翻译的时候可以根据笔记和记忆适当的调整词汇出现的顺序或语序，例如“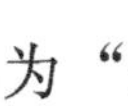”译为“全球市场”，而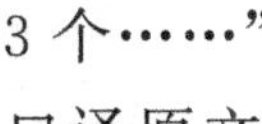则可以先将“”译出，为“全球范围内有 8 个……3 个……”。

下文的口译原文节选自国家能源局油气司司长张玉清在 2010 年 6 月北京举办的第二届中国石油石化产业发展国际论坛的致辞。口译笔记与译文为笔者所写所译，仅供参考。

节选内容	口译笔记	译文
尊敬的石油界的各位老领导，各位嘉宾，女士们、先生们，朋友们，大家下午好！很高兴参加第二届中国石油石化产业发展国际论坛”，首先对本次论坛的召开表示热烈祝贺！	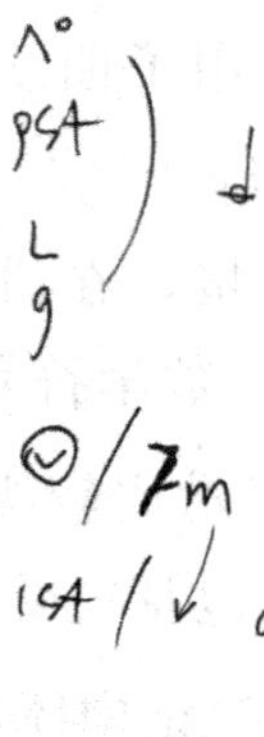	Honored leaders in oil industry, distinguished guests, ladies and gentlemen, good afternoon. I'm glad to attend the 2nd China petroleum and petrochemical industry development International Forum. First, I would like to extend my warm congratulations on the opening of the forum.
能源是人类社会赖以生存和发展的重要基础，也是生产力发展的动力源泉。进入工业化以来，人类使用能源，特别是化学能源的数量越来越多，同时也带来了一些环境和气候问题。目前世界各国纷纷制定发展清洁能源、低碳排放的新能源政策。	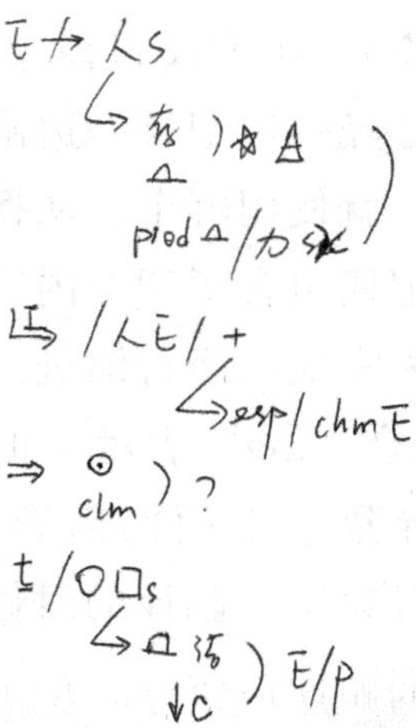	Energy is the important basis of human society for its existence and development, and also the source of power for productivity growth. Since the industrialization, people use more and more energy, especially chemical energy, which results in some environmental and climate problems. At present, countries around the world have made new energy policies involving developing clean energy and low carbon emission.

续表

节选内容	口译笔记	译文
石油天然气作为化石能源，如何在低碳、清洁能源发展大潮中发挥应有的作用，也成为摆在我们面前的重大课题。我们期待各位专家在《中国石油石化》杂志社打造的这个交流平台上，分享低碳经济企业家和专家的经验，促进石油石化行业健康发展。最后，预祝本次论坛获得圆满成功。谢谢大家！	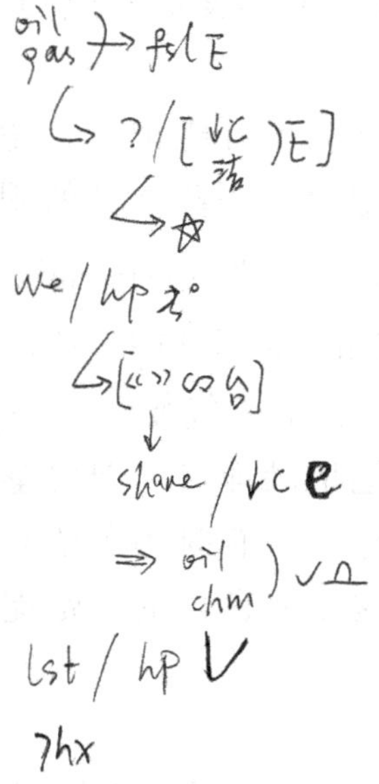	As fossil energy, how petroleum and natural gas play their parts in the stream of developing low carbon and clean energy has also become a key issue that we should face. We hope all experts and entrepreneurs can share your experiences in low carbon economy so as to facilitate the sound development of petroleum and petrochemical industry. Last, may the forum a great success. Thank you.

口译笔记一为典型的大会致辞开头的笔记，包括对不同参与人的称呼，然后表示欢迎或祝贺。所有称呼并列向下一一列出，笔记仅仅列出称呼，至于称呼前的敬语一般脑记或遵从约定俗成的用法。“”表示“下午好”（good afternoon）。笑脸符号“”表示“高兴”（glad，delighted…）。节选二包括三个句子，在口译笔记二中表现得很明显。笔记中包含了很多符号，“”表示“发展”（development），“”表示“重要的”（important），“”表示“基础”（basis），“”表示“环境”（environment），“”表示“各个，全部”（every，all），“”表示“国家”（country，nation，state），后面加“s”表示复数。口译笔记三包含了三方面的内容。两次使用中

括号，“[]”里的内容一般为状语或介词短语，表示条件、地点、时间等。英文字母“E”表示“能源”（energy），“e”表示“经济”（economy），“V”表示“成功，胜利”（success, victory）。

综上所述，交替传译离不开笔记，清楚详尽的笔记是高质量译文的有力保障。笔记包括一些常见的固定使用的缩写和符号，包括“口”（国家），“esp”（especially）等，同时还包括一些译员临时想出来的缩写和符号，例如“б”表示“breakthrough”，“clm”表示“气候”等。然而，交替传译离不开大脑记忆，在对照笔记翻译时，要将笔记中的缩写和符号还原成语言，即译成目标语，有时为了语言完整还要译一些笔记上没有记录的内容，这需要良好的记忆能力。

四、论坛口译的收尾阶段

对于口译员而言，论坛结束并不意味着口译工作的完结，由于每次论坛的主题不同，发言人不同，因此每次论坛口译对译员来说都是一次成长和提高。论坛结束后，译员一般要做以下工作。第一，对于论坛上遇到的专业术语、出现的新的语言点进行总结。作为口译员，要时刻保持学习的状态，日常生活中遇到新词热词要记忆，在每次做完会议口译后，更要将会议上出现的专有名词、术语、搭配或口译搭档使用较好的表达方式记录下来，让他们成为自己知识的一部分。第二，对论坛相关资料进行归类整理。会议或论坛的译员一般有自己擅长的领域，为什么鲜有译员能够胜任所有领域的口译呢？究其原因主要是因为每个领域都有本领域内的概念、理论、实践方法等。隔行如隔山，尽管不要求译员完全了解一个领域后再做这个领域的翻译，但是仍要掌握一些基本知识，这对译员在翻译时进行理解、预测有极大的帮助。整理论坛资料是了解一个领域最快捷的方式，因为论坛上邀请的都是行业的领军人物，他们的发言都代表了这个行业的发展前沿与亟待解决的重大问题。伟大头脑思想的碰撞不仅仅对于增长见识，对于提高智慧、改善思维模式也是极其有益的。

论坛结束后，译员除了自我总结外，还要接受评估。论坛举办方会对译员所属公司或译员本人就译员在论坛上的表现以及论坛参加者对译员的评价进行反馈。这些意见或建议对译员意义重大，一方面决定了译员的报酬以及在这个行业的声誉，另一方面指明了译员的优缺点，以及未来努力的方向。

口译已经成为任何大型国际论坛、会议必不可少的一部分。论坛口译增强了国际交流，让一个国家、一个企业、一个组织的声音让世界都听到。论坛口译已经成为当今炙手可热的行业，亟待更多人才的加入。

附录一
网站信息翻译纠错解析

如果有外国企业或公司网站的中文版语句不通、词不达意、错别字连篇，我们会怎样看待？我们在买这家企业或公司的产品时，会不会迟疑？我们的跨国公司或产品出口企业一般有英文网站，或是网站的英文版，是否也存在这种现象？此处以英文网站实际错误案例分析的方式就编译技巧的应用予以具体指导，以期在工作中规避类似问题，有效维护企业或公司的对外形象。

一、数字翻译错误

如果企业或公司的中期报告、年度报告等，数字错了，可能会影响投资者信心，股价大跌。数字一般都是阿拉伯字，不存在翻译困难的问题，但在下例子中我们发现中文数字的意义和英文数字的意义相差甚远了，“270，000”意为“27 万”，而英文里却加了个“million”。例如：

实现世界上单套能力最大的年产27 万吨生物柴油加工装置（FAME）试车一次成功；

We succeeded in the trial production of biodiesel at a FAME processing facility, which has the world's highest production capacity for a single facility and a design capacity of *270,000 million* tonnes per annum.

二、单词拼写错误

英文的拼写错误类似汉字的错别字，写字时多了一撇或少了一点，在英文拼写单词时多了个字母或少了个字母，英文叫“typo”，或是“incorrect spelling”，据说，这两者是有区别的，“typo”是不小心输错了，而“incorrect spelling”是学艺不精，记单词时就记错了。不管怎样，用电脑输入或编辑，类似下例中“*Maccala*”这种错误是完全可以避免的。正确拼写为“Malacca”。

马六甲油田生产的原油3万吨运抵南京，这是中国产自国外运回国内的第一船油。

The shipment of 30, 000 tons of crude oil produced from Maccala Strait arrived Nanjing. This is the first shipment of crude oil produced from overseas for China.

三、误用无关别字

中文汉字的别字通常是张冠李戴，主要原因有三种：一是由于形似，如“松弛”误作“松驰”；二是由于同音，如“提纲”误作“题纲”；三是由于义近，如“擅长”误作“善长”。

而英文的别字似乎多因形似而错用，下例中将“pearl”写成了“pear”、将“plaque”写成了“plague”。

> ... singed a PSC with Devon Energy Corporation (Devon, NYSE: DVN) for deepwater block 42/05 in the *Pear* River Mouth Basin of South China Sea.
>
> In 2012, we won the Lifeline Express 15th Anniversary Special Award, and were among the first batch of companies, to be honoured with an appreciation *plague* from China Women ' s Development Foundation (CWDF) ...

四、错用标点符号

不管英文里是否有这种标点符号，就直接把中文的标点符号，如书名号、顿号搬到英文里了。其实，在纯英文状态下可以检测判断英文里是不是有某种标点符号，直接用键盘可以输入的，便是英文的标点符号。下例中在英文表达中用书名号是不符合英文标点使用规则的。

> 国务院发布《中华人民共和国对外合作开采海洋石油资源条例》，确定了海上对外合作第一轮国际招标的《标准合同》。
>
> The 《 Regulations of People ' s Republic of

China Concerning the Exploitation of The Offshore Petroleum Resources in Cooperation with Foreign Enterprises》 was promulgated by the State Council. The《Model Contract》for the first round of international bidding for the offshore cooperation with foreign enterprises was finalized.

五、用词专业性弱

如果对船舶有点了解，会知道"barge"指的驳船。《柯林斯英汉双解大词典》给出的定义是：

> *N－COUNT* A barge is a long, narrow boat with a flat bottom. Barges are used for carrying heavy loads, especially on rivers and canals.

即"平底载货船"。因此，下例中的"起重船"用"barge"显然不合适。

> ……公司和……重工集团有限公司举行深水铺管起重船工程项目船舶建造合同签约仪式。
>
> ... Company and ... Heavy Industry Corporation signed an agreement for the construction of a deepwater pipe-laying crane barge.

直接搜索"深水铺管起重船"，会找到很多论文，其中有篇《HYSY201深水铺管起重船吊机旋转平衡系统制造工艺》,[①] 里面有英文摘要，用的是 vessel。还可以搜索 deepwater pipe laying crane vessel，能找到国外的报道，说明这样翻译是靠谱的。

“机械完工”是个术语，用来描述工程项目达到某个进度和状态，中文里要加动词“达到”才更加明确。在百度输入“机械完工”，第一个结果就是百度百科关于“机械完工”的词条——机械完工（Mechanical Completion，MC），是国际认可并广泛使用的工程完工报检机制，是船舶及海上平台调试之前的一个重要部分。目的是对海洋工程和船舶某个系统、设备的安装工作进行详细的完整性检查，从而确认系统、设备的安装符合项目要求，及相关图纸和规格书的要求，并处于安全的调试状态，为与调试、调试做好充分的准备工作。[②] 搜索“Mechanical Completion”，有个网站给出的定义是：

> Unit is essentially complete for start-up operation and test run. All major work is completed. Minor work not interfering with operation may not be completed, such as punch list and minor touch-up work. [③]

搜索网页、图片、论文、中英文百科和法规，可以帮助我们查清楚各种专业术语的中英文名称、定义，避免错误。例

---

① http：//wenku. baidu. com/link? url =-U1b3ajVOJSvAbXVmipzIVTeq CZw7qYTfd2sI5BKYOi3FV48oZ7CXJOIQ40rihRVajJpxbL5QHjXndu8uOQd87cr61ZWsgTEDmmG4MzJDPG.

② http：//baike. baidu. com/item/%E6%9C%BA%E6%A2%B0%E5%AE%8C%E5%B7%A5? fr=aladdin.

③ http：//www. dictionaryofconstruction. com/definition/mechanical-completion. html.

如：

“XX 25-1 南”天然气利用项目机械完工。

XX 25-1 South natural gas utilization project completed the mechanic work.

六、臆造英文词句

若加玻纤或阻燃，可特别订制超强耐磨，耐腐蚀性的专用料管。

If glass fibre or *thermoresist* is added, they can be used to manufacture special usage piles which are highly resistance to erosion and scraping.

“thermoresist”似乎是编译者制造出来的英文单词，由“thermo”（热、热电）和 resist（抵抗，反抗，抗，忍得住，抗蚀剂，保护层）组成。词典里类似的词不少，如：“burning resistance”（耐燃性），“flame proof”（耐火性），“flame resistivity”（阻焰性，耐火性），“flame retardant plastic”（防火塑料），“flame retarding polymer”（阻燃聚合物），“flame-retardant”（阻燃的）。即便这样，抗热或是耐热和阻燃意思也是不同的。“thermoresist”一词应改成“flame-retardant material”。

管理理念：一次做对做好，零缺陷管理，可靠性保证。

Our management philosophy: finish tasks perfectly once, zero error management, ensure a high creditability.

上面例子中引用了克劳士比（Philip B. Crosby，1926－2001）的管理理念。原本的说法是：

Do it right the first time. Zero Defects.

第一次就把事情做对。零缺陷。

最好不自造英文词句。

七、忽略文化差异

天将降大任于斯人也，必先苦其心志，劳其筋骨，饿其体肤，空乏其身，行拂乱其所为。

When Heaven is about to place a great responsibility on a great man, it always first frustrates his spirit and will, exhausts his muscles and bones, exposes him to starvation and poverty, harasses him by troubles and setbacks so as to stimulate his spirit, toughen his nature and enhance his abilities.

上面例句中的中文部分没什么问题，每个受过教育的中国人都能大概理解这句话的含义，即使不知道是孟子说的。但是，在英文网站上这样直接翻出来，外国人会觉得很突兀。建议前面加上一段解释：

Mencius, a great philosopher in the fourth century B. C. E. , said:

公元前四世纪的伟大哲学家孟子说过：

几点建议：

第一，重视网站英文版的翻译。

英文版当然是给不懂中文懂英文的顾客或潜在顾客看的。看看老外怎么说：

Western Customers judge whether they want to buy from you based on your initial sales copy. Proper grammar and writing skills are critically important.

西方客户是否买你的东西，首先基于对你销售文案的判断。正确的语法和写作技巧是至关重要的。

If your sales copy contains English mistakes then buyers automatically assume that your Company produces poor products. They will also view you as being unprofessional and prone to mistakes in your business. You will never hear from them, but your competitors will.

如果你的销售文案有英文错误，买家自然会假设你们公司生产劣质产品。他们还会认为你不够专业、容易在业务上犯错。他们不会再来找你，而是去找你的竞争者。

第二，留意中西文化差异。

大多数公司的英文网站是按照中文网站翻译的，似乎无可厚非，但实际上中西文化的差异是很大的。我们关心的，人家可能不在乎；而人家重视的，我们又没说到。例如：西方大公司网站大多会提到公司“使命”（mission）“愿景”（vision）“核心价值观”（core value），而中国人常说“注册资本”“高级职称”“大专学历以上占员工总数的百分数”等。不敢说谁对谁错、谁高谁低，主要是文化差异。因此，建议做英文网站翻译时，参考地道的英文网站，[1] 不要简单地中翻英。

① 例如：http：//corporate. exxonmobil. com，http：//www. bp. com，http：//www. shell. com，http：//www. conocophillips. com，http：//www. slb. com，http：//www. halliburton. com.

附录二
辅助会议速记的软硬件工具

一、语音识别系统

随着计算机处理能力的迅速提高，20 世纪 70 年代开始，IBM 公司致力于设计一个语音打印机，即把讲话者的内容转换成文字显示或打印在纸上，20 世纪 90 年代该项技术从实验室走向应用，用语音来实现人与计算机之间的交互，即让计算机能“听懂”人类语言，与此同时，人们将识别准确率纳入语音识别技术评估机制中。

语音识别技术主要涉及语音识别（auto speech recognition）、自然语言理解（natural language understanding）以及语音合成（speech synthesis）等三项内容。

语音识别系统本身是一种模式识别系统，基本单元有：（1）特征参数提取—识别系统输入端，具体过程是：未知（待识别）语音→语音信号（通过话筒转化为电信号）；（2）模式匹配—语音识别模板，具体过程是：输入语音参数与计算机语音模板参数比对分析→搜索和匹配策略；（3）参考模式库，特征选择与最优动态规整水平、语音模板优劣、模板准确率高低是该系统应用效果的核心。同一个音由不同的人发出或同一个人在不同时刻发出，不可能具有完全相同的时间长度，因此不能简单地将语音参数与模板参数匹配。日本学者板仓提出的动态规整技术，采用一种最优化算法“动态规整法”，这是一种将时间规整和距离测度有机结合在一起的非线性规整技术，保证了待识别特征与模板特征之间最大的声学相似性和最小的时差失真。

（一）基于非特定人工作方式的 UniLite 语音识别芯片

非特定人工作方式的 UniLite 语音识别芯片采用基于统计模型的算法，芯片开发者事先采集大量的语音数据进行训练，建立声学模型。在识别阶段，机器将用户的输入语音特征与通过声学模型构建的识别网络进行匹配解码，得到识别结果。对用户来讲，不需要引入烦琐的训练过程，同时还可供不同的人使用。非特定人识别芯片的词条数量可达上千万，识别性能不会随着识别词条数目的增加有明显的下降，并具有一定的抗噪能力。UniLite 语音识别芯片具有识别性能高和识别响应时间迅速等优势。此外，UniLite 语音识别芯片可储存多个识别词表，支持每次识别动态制定 Active 词表；支持每次识别动态传送 Active 词表，或对指定的某个已存储词表附加动态传送的 Active 词条。中文语音识别中，UniLite 语音识别芯片在无须借助 PC 等任何外部资源及额外训练环节与时间等情况下，支持识别词表的实时更新，并在下一次识别中生效。

（二）Nuance 语音识别软件

"Nuance Communications"是一家语音及图像解决方案提供商，是全球最大的专业从事语音识别软件研发及销售的公司，此外，公司还研发多款输入法软件等产品。Nuance 语音识别软件提供了一种方便优化、高度准确和易于配置的可扩展语音解决方案。Nuance 语音识别软件由 Nuance 基础 API、语音模板库、编辑服务器、语音服务器和后台运行数据库等构成。Nuance 语音识别软件支持自然、自由的语音识别，识别率一般不低于 98%；支持基于开放标准的语音应用编辑语言，如 VoiceXML2.0；具有自动调效功能，即自行调整以适应特定用户群的共同特征（可将错误率降低至60%）；可处理一亿条语法；强噪环境下识别准确率高；能将语音识别、声纹识别和语音合成无缝集成。

（三）IBM-ViaVoice和Windows-Vista语音识别系统

IBM-ViaVoice和Windows-Vista语音识别系统可以帮助用户以口述的方式编写文本——“听写到语音板”。这两种语音识别系统对个人计算机硬盘空间要求比较高，安装过程略显比较复杂。此外，因其抗噪效果比较弱，用户要为系统配置质量较好的耳麦，还需要建立个人语音模型，提高辨识准确效果，发挥错误辨识功能。

辅助英语速记的语音识别软硬件工具的功能有：

- 英语声音内容（可视听）直接生成转化为英文文本内容（可阅读）；
- 在英语词库模式下，输入英语词语的首尾字母（或字母组合）后，计算机即可呈现出相关英语词语的列表；
- 在英语词库模式下，计算机可按文章中选定词语的出现频率并排序，生成英语关键词词语的列表。

二、文语转换系统

文语转换系统（text to speech，TTS）即把计算机文本转换为连续自然的语音流，是CTI（computer telecommunication integration）技术的一个方面，是语音合成技术的重要延伸。国内主要产品有捷通华声的jTTS SDK工具包。利用此开发包，可使计算机像人一样将提供的文字通过放音设备读出来，或转化为wav及其他格式的语音文件以便储存。jTTS支持中英文混读，更适用于现代文本阅读。它具有连续流畅、自然度高、音库大小可调节、音色可转换等特点。

辅助英语速记的文语转换软硬件工具应能完成英文文本内容（可阅读）直接生成转化为英语声音内容（可视听）。功能表现在：

• 浏览word文本格式的文本，可编辑、修改和排版

• 在文本编辑界面中有“合成”按钮，启动语音合成模块，自动合成语音拼读英文；

• 对合成的语音能生成音频文件并保存，也能打开播放。

三、文字书写工具

目前，国内手写输入工具的代表产品是汉王笔，一般由手写板（后置有与电脑连接的接口）和电脑笔（无线无源压感笔）两部分组成。电脑笔通过运笔的轻重缓急表现笔记的粗细浓淡，与支持压感技术的Photoshop、Painter、Flash和Photoimpact等绘图软件兼容。汉王笔拥有近三万字符的字库，可连续输入行草连笔字、英文、数字、符号（近3万种）等，在无须切换界面的情况下一笔写到底，正确率高，还可直接对PPT、WORD、EXCEL等文件进行批注，勾画出示意图标注重点，遇到会读不会写的字词，可通过书写同音字词找到，在电子公文交转中可完成签名。汉王笔系统设置包括识别

设置（词语联想、笔势识别、手写习惯调节）、手写设置（笔迹颜色、笔迹粗细、笔迹类型）、颜色设置（色彩方案）、发音设置（音速、音质）、笔势浏览（退格、空格、删除、回车）和工具箱等六个部分。

四、文字修订系统

Windows 中的 Word 软件里包括了修订功能。这里主要介绍一下 Markin[①] 工具。

Markin 中包括标注语法错误、拼写错误、词序错误及其他普遍存在的错误。它所使用的缩写对大多数人来说都是比较熟悉的（如“sp”代表拼写），而对于不同类型的错误它会用不同的颜色标示出来。这对于日常工作中的专业速记人员是必要的，但要注意选择美式英语检查还是英式英语检查。对初学者来说，使用拼写检查工具可以引起其对自己的错误更清楚，还有机会去修改错误。此外，文字处理软件还包括字典、语法和同义词库工具。如鼠标放在“happy”上，同义词库即列出诸如“content”“glad”“cheerful”等同义词，这样有益于扩大词汇量，但要注意词语意义及用法的准确性。总之，利用上述工具开展记笔记及笔记修改活动有助于速记者创造性地使用语言完成信息速记。

① http：//www. cict. co. uk/software/markin/index. htm.

附录三
OPEC组织相关信息资料

一、简介

石油输出国组织（Organization of Petroleum Exporting Countries，OPEC）。成立于1960年9月14日，1962年11月6日OPEC在联合国秘书处备案，成为正式的国际组织。其宗旨是协调和统一成员国的石油政策，维护各自的和共同的利益。现有12个成员国：沙特阿拉伯、伊拉克、伊朗、科威特、阿拉伯联合酋长国、卡塔尔、利比亚、尼日利亚、阿尔及利亚、安哥拉、厄瓜多尔和委内瑞拉。

石油输出国组织总部自1965年9月起，由瑞士日内瓦迁往奥地利首都维也纳。石油输出国组织是第三世界建立最早、影响最大的原料生产国和输出组织。石油是战后世界最主要的能源。战后初期，世界石油的勘探、开采和销售几乎全部控制在西方石油垄断财团手中。这个垄断控制的后果是西方发达国家获得超额利润，第三世界主要产油国的经济利益却受到损害。为了抗衡主要油公司（大多为美资、英资和德资），借以降低油价和生产者的负担。最初组织只是一个非官方的议价小组借以减价销售至第三世界国家。20世纪70年代初期OPEC开始展露其效用。

以巴冲突的出现终于引致OPEC由一个单纯的企业联合转型为一股不容忽视的政治力量。1967年，第三次中东战争后，OPEC的阿拉伯成员国成立另一个重叠的组织，名为“阿拉伯石油输出国家组织”（Organisation of Arab Petroleum Exporting Countries，OAPEC），来集中向支持以色列的西方施压。就算不是主要石油输出国的埃及和叙利亚亦也加入了阿拉伯石油输出国家组织，以协助达成其目标。其后，1973 年赎罪日战争的爆发更坚固了阿拉伯国家的这个选择。由于美国对以色列的紧急补给，使以军能抵挡住埃及和叙利亚军队，愤怒的阿拉伯世界于 1973 年对美国、西欧和日本实施石油禁运，使 20 世纪 70 年代初期，西方大型的石油企业集团突然面对一批联合的产油国。

二、创建背景

作为发展中国家建立最早、影响最大的原料生产国与输出国组织，OPEC 的诞生并非偶然，而是战后亚非拉民族解放运动蓬勃高涨的历史产物，是发展中国家在国际舞台上崛起的标志性事件。

OPEC 由中东海湾的沙特、科威特、伊朗、伊拉克以及拉美的委内瑞拉等 5 个石油出口国于 1960 年 9 月在巴格达发起组成。这五个 OPEC 创始国石油资源不但储量极其丰富，而且油田分布集中，开采条件好，成本低、利润高。从 20 世纪初到二战前，它们就是国际石油资本竞相角逐的重点对象。二战后，以“七姐妹”[①] 为代表的西方国际石油卡特尔加速对这些国家的石油开发。这 5 国的探明剩余可采石油储量在 1945～1960年的 15 年里以年均 29.1％的速度增长了 4.37 倍，

① 由美国、英国和荷兰垄断资本控制的七家大石油公司（美国的埃克森公司、德士古公司、莫比尔石油公司、加利福尼亚标准石油公司、海湾石油公司，英国与荷兰合资的英荷壳牌石油公司，英国石油公司）组成的国际石油卡特尔的别称。

占全球石油储量的比重由原来的 56.8% 增加到 1960 年的 66.67%；而它们的石油出口更是由 1951 年的 1.3898 亿吨增长到 1960 年的 3.1039 亿吨，占 1960 年世界石油出口总量的 81.43%。以这些 OPEC 创始国为代表的亚非拉产油国尽管石油资源丰富，但“七姐妹”等西方国际石油资本长期控制着国际石油市场的勘探、开采、运输、精练直至销售各环节，特别是它们拥有对亚非拉产油国石油的定价权和经营权，从中获得源源不断的廉价石油，使西方发达国家迅速在能源领域以油代煤的转变过程中实现了战后经济的高速增长。而亚非拉产油国却在它们的长期盘剥、掠夺下资源毁耗、经济畸形、政局动荡，债台高筑。同时，二战前作为世界主要石油输出国的美国在战后已变成原油输入国，它和西欧、日本一起构成对这些中东及拉美产油国石油输出的严重依赖。正是这种日益加深的严重依赖，使得 5 大产油国在世界石油市场上控制着绝对的份额，并以绝对优势的地位创立了石油输出国组织。

OPEC 的形成与战后中东阿拉伯民族主义运动的振兴直接有关。1945 年阿拉伯国家联盟（简称阿盟）成立后，为协调阿拉伯国家的石油政策，于 1952 年在阿盟政治委员会中设立了“石油专家委员会”，1954 年又设立永久性机构“石油局”，以争取和捍卫阿拉伯世界的石油权益。

OPEC 成立的直接诱因是以“七姐妹”为代表的西方石油垄断资本单方面连续压低原油价格。二战后特别是 50 年代，随着中东石油大量开采，国际石油市场供过于求，独立石油公司和苏联为打进西方国际石油卡特尔控制的世界市场，纷纷降价抛售石油。西方国际石油卡特尔不甘心让出市场份额，1959 年 2 月英国石油公司（BP）遂宣布每桶原油削价 18 美分。这次削价使中东产油国石油收入顿减 10%。同年 4 月阿盟在开罗举行第一届阿拉伯石油大会，除阿拉伯产油国外，还有非阿拉伯世界的伊朗和委内瑞拉两大产油国以观察员身份出席此次会议。会议强烈谴责西方国际石油卡特尔单方面强行压价，要求西方石油大公司稳定油价，即使不得已调整油价，也需事先与产油国协商。期间沙特与委内瑞拉还达成了成立石油输出国组织以稳定油价的“君子协定”。1960 年 5 月沙特石油事务大臣塔里基和委内瑞拉石油部长在举行会谈后发表公报，明确提出建立石油输出国组织的倡议。但 1960 年 8 月埃克森再次将每桶中东原油削价 10 美分。随后其他大石油公司也采取类似行动。这两次削价使 OPEC 中的 4 个中东创始国每年石油收入损失 2.31 亿美元。为摆脱任凭西方石油垄断资本随意宰割的状况，1960 年 9 月 9～14 日，沙特、科威特、伊朗、伊拉克以及拉美的委内瑞拉等 5 个石油出口国在巴格达召开会议，决定联合起来共同对付西方国际石油卡特尔，以维护产油国合理的石油权益。

1960 年 9 月 14 日由上述 5 国创立的石油输出国组织的主要宗旨是：“协调和统一各成员国的石油政策和确定最有效的手段，单独地、集体地维护成员国的利益”，“应设法确保国际石油市场价格的稳定，以避免有害的和不必要的波动影响本组织。”由此，一个协调成员国石油政策、谋求合理的民族经济权益、反对西方国际石油垄断资本掠夺和控制的发展中国家原料生产与输出国国际组织正式亮相于国际舞台。

1961 年至 1975 年，又有亚、非、拉 8 个产油国先后加入 OPEC：卡塔尔（1961 年）、印度尼西亚（1962 年）、利比亚（1962 年）、阿联酋（1967 年）、阿尔及利亚（1969 年）及尼日利亚（1971 年）；此外，厄瓜多尔（1973 年）和加蓬（1975 年）加入 OPEC 后又于分别 1992 年和 1995 年退出。

阿拉伯产油国认为，除 OPEC 之外，还有必要建立一个完全由阿拉伯国家组成的石油联合组织，来统一和协调阿拉伯产油国之间的石油政策。1968 年 1 月，沙特阿拉伯、科威特和利比亚在发起成立了阿拉伯石油输出国组织（简称“欧阿佩克”），随后，除阿曼和突尼斯外，几乎所有的阿拉伯产油国都先后加入。

三、目标宗旨

OPEC 的成立宗旨是：

协调并统一成员国的石油政策；讨论并决定为保护成员国利益而采取的单独或联合的最佳方式；通过消除危害性价格波动从而保证国际市场石油价格的稳定；保证产油国收入的持续稳定；保证对石油消费国高效、经济及有序的供给；保证石油工业有一个平衡的收入。

四、组织架构

1961 年 OPEC 在委内瑞拉的加拉加斯召开了第二次会议，其主要目的就是明确章程和组织机构的形式，其机构包括：大会、理事会（主席兼秘书长）秘书处。大会为该组织的最高权力机构；理事会负责行政管理及贯彻执行大会的各项决议。OPEC 的机构和章程曾于 1965 年做过重新修订，修订的结果是秘书处的职能得到强化，并与理事会分开，故而OPEC仅前两位理事会主席兼任过秘书长。

（一）OPEC大会

OPEC大会是该组织的最高权力机构，各成员国向大会派出以石油、矿产和能源部长（大臣）为首的代表团。大会每年召开两次，如有需要还可召开特别会议。大会奉行全体成员国一致原则，每个成员国均为一票，负责制定该组织的大政方针，并决定以何种适当方式加以执行。

OPEC大会同时还决定是否接纳新的成员国，审议理事会就该组织事务提交的报告和建议。大会审议通过对来自任何一个成员国的理事的任命，并选举理事会主席。大会有权要求理事会就涉及该组织利益的任何事项提交报告或提出建议。大会还要对理事会提交的OPEC预算报告加以审议，并决定是否进行修订。

（二）OPEC理事会

OPEC理事会类似于普通商业机构的理事会，由各成员国提名并经大会通过的理事组成，每两年为一届。理事会负责管理OPEC的日常事务，执行大会决议，起草年度预算报告，并提交给大会审议通过。理事会还审议由秘书长向大会提交的有关OPEC日常事务的报告。

（三）OPEC秘书处

OPEC秘书处依据《OPEC组织条例》，在理事会的领导下负责行使该组织的行政性职能。秘书处由秘书长、调研室、数据服务中心、能源形势研究部门、石油市场分析部门、行政与人事部门、信息部门、秘书长办公室以及法律室组成。秘书处 1961 年设立，办公地点最初在日内瓦，后来由于瑞士方面拒绝为 OPEC 提供任何的外交及其他方面的优惠或特权，OPEC 又将其总部迁至维也纳。秘书处内设有一专门机构——经济委员会，协助该组织把国际石油价格稳定在公平合理的水平上。

五、加入条件

《OPEC 组织条例》规定：

> 在根本利益上与各成员国相一致、确实可实现原油净出口的任何国家，在为全权成员国的三分之二多数接纳，并为所有创始成员国一致接纳后，可成为本组织的全权成员国。

该组织条例进一步区分了三类成员国的范畴：

- 创始成员国——1960 年 9 月出席在伊拉克首都巴格达举行的 OPEC 第一次会议，并签署成立 OPEC 原始协议的国家；
- 全权成员国——包括创始成员国以及加入 OPEC 的申请已为大会所接受的所有国家；
- 准成员国——虽未获得全权成员国的资格，但在大会规定的特殊情况下仍为大会所接纳的国家。

六、运营方式

OPEC各成员国的代表（主要是代表团团长）在OPEC大会上对其石油政策加以协调、统一，以促进石油市场的稳定与繁荣。OPEC秘书处负责该组织的日常事务，接受理事会的指令，由秘书长直接领导。OPEC下设的经济委员会、部长监察委员会等多个执行机构，则履行咨询、磋商、协调等多项职能。

OPEC成员国对当前形势和市场走向加以分析预测，明确经济增长速率和石油供求状况等多项基本因素，然后据此磋商在其石油政策中进行何种调整。例如，在以往数次大会中，OPEC成员国曾分别确定提高或是减少该组织的总体石油产量，以便维持石油价格的稳定，为消费国提供稳定的短期、中期乃至长期的石油供应。

OPEC组织在近年曾多次使得石油价格暴涨来抗衡美国等西方发达国家。为平衡世界力量有不可小觑的作用。

组织成员国共控制约全球2/3的石油贮备，约共占世界石油蕴藏78%以上的石油储量并提供40%以上的石油消费量。它们占全球产油量的40%和出口量的50%。因此，OPEC成员国得以从石油出口得到更多收益。

由于石油销售被美元所主导，美元兑其他货币的汇率会直接影响OPEC对石油的定价。举例说，当美元对其他货币下跌，OPEC成员国会收取较少的其他货币。因为它们持续以美元出售石油，这将导致美元购买力直接的下降。当欧元引入后，伊拉克决定以欧元代替美元作为出售石油的交易货币。

OPEC 的决定相当影响国际油价。例如，于 1973 年石油危机，OPEC 拒绝运送石油至于赎罪日战争（十月战争）支持以列对抗埃及和叙利亚的西方国家。这使油价上升 4 倍，从 1973 年 10 月 17 日至 1974 年 3 月 18 日，持续 5 个月之久。于 1975 年 1 月 7 日，OPEC 成员国同意将原油价格提高 10%。与此同时，OPEC 成员国（包括一些刚把石油工业国有化的国家）响应国际新经济秩序的呼吁。在阿尔及尔举行的 OPEC 第一次高峰会，它呼吁定下稳定而合理的物价、国际食物和农业计划、由南至北的技术转移，及经济系统的民主。

与其他的企业协议不同，OPEC 成功将油价持续上升。OPEC 的成功大部分都归功于沙特阿拉伯的弹性。该国容许其他参与协议国家的欺诈，更减少自己的产量来弥补其他成员超出配额的生产。因为其他的成员均全力生产，而沙特阿拉伯是唯一的成员拥有充裕的贮存空间，亦有在需要时增产的能力，这给予它们可靠的杠杆效应。

这个政策十分成功，导致原油价格一度上升至仅次于提炼油产品的水平。然而 OPEC 提高价格的能力亦受一些限制。油价上升会使消费下跌、收益下跌。而且价格持续上升会鼓励根本性的行为转变，比如替代能源的利用或者节约能源的推广。

伊拉克前总统萨达姆·侯赛因提倡 OPEC 提高油价，以协助伊拉克及其他成员国支付债务的利息，引致 1990—1991 年海湾战争的爆发。但两伊战争和海湾战争惹起 OPEC 成员国的分歧，使这段时期成为 OPEC 成员间内聚力达至低点。一旦中断供应的担心，伴随这些冲突消散，油价就开始下滑。

当油价跌至约 10 美元一桶，经委内瑞拉总统查韦斯·弗里亚斯的外交斡旋后，成功协调于 1998 年开始恢复按比例产油。2000 年，查韦斯主持 OPEC 成立 25 周年的成员国元首高峰会。2004 年 8 月，OPEC 开始传出其成员国只有少量的增产能力，显示出 OPEC 对原油价格的影响力逐渐消失。印尼的被迫退出也正因为印尼已非石油净输出国亦没有足够的能力达致其产量配额。

七、成员国关系

在制定石油政策时，在抑制过高油价的问题上，OPEC 成员国因国情不同存在很大争议。基于石油政策立场上的不同，人们一般将 OPEC 成员国划分为以沙特等国为代表的“鸽派”和以伊朗等国为代表的“鹰派”。“鸽派”和“鹰派”的称呼源于油价政策上的差异，“鸽派”国家在目标油价的设定上态度较为温和，认为油价应该缓慢上涨，而“鹰派”国家则主张石油价格应该大幅提高。其实，价格主张上的差异只是一种表面现象。两类国家立场的不同实际是源于国家目标的差异。“鸽派”国家石油资源丰富，又不需要大笔资金支持国内建设，其油价政策往往是基于长远考虑，将油价维持在合理区间。而“鹰派”国家需要大笔资金支持国内建设，而其产量却难以提高，因此，在制定石油政策时，“更希望维持高油价，获得更多石油收入”。在产量方面，“鹰派”国家一般会选择开足马力进行生产，而“鸽派”国家则会通过产量调整稳定油价。

其实，OPEC1980 年通过的《石油长期战略问题报告书》明确提出了以通胀率、汇率和经合组织成员国经济增长率调整油价的原则。但却因为“鹰派”国家在油价政策上的强硬立场，各项原则最终没有实现。实际上，从20世纪70年代中期到80年代中期，OPEC很多政策的推出都是“鸽派”和“鹰派”之间相互交锋和妥协的结果。不过，作为“卡特尔”，OPEC通过产量调整来影响油价，剩余产能的不同也就决定了OPEC成员国之间实力上的差异。在OPEC国家中，“鸽派”国家握有剩余产能，具备调节产量的能力，而“鹰派”国家产量调节能力有限。因此，“鸽派”国家在OPEC石油政策的制定中占有主动。“鹰派”国家只能通过向“鸽派”国家，特别是沙特阿拉伯施加压力（也就是迫使沙特等国减产）来实现自己的高油价政策。

在20世纪七八十年代，OPEC“鹰派”国家，特别是伊朗、伊拉克还能凭借强大的政治、军事实力迫使沙特等国接受自己主张。但1980年两伊战争和1991年海湾战争的接连爆发却导致OPEC“鹰派”国家的地区影响力急剧下降。以沙特为代表的“鸽派”国家实际上成为80年代中期之后OPEC石油政策的主导者。

八、组织成员

OPEC的发起国为伊拉克、伊朗、科威特、沙特阿拉伯、委内瑞拉，它们都是1960年9月即第一次OPEC大会上就成为成员国的即创始成员国。

除上述五国外，OPEC的全权成员国还有：卡塔尔（1961年1月第二届大会），印度尼西亚（1962—2009年），利比亚

（1962 年 6 月第四届大会），阿拉伯联合酋长国（1967 年 12 月第十四届大会），阿尔及利亚（1969 年 7 月第十八届大会），尼日利亚（1971 年 7 月第二十四届大会），厄瓜多尔（1973 年 11 月第三十六届大会加入，1992 年退出，2007 年重新加入），加蓬（1975—1994 年），安哥拉（2007 年 1 月 1 日）。

截至目前，OPEC 共有 12 个成员国。

（一）沙特阿拉伯（Kingdom of Saudi Arabia）

沙特阿拉伯王国位于阿拉伯半岛。东濒波斯湾，西临红海，同约旦、伊拉克、科威特、阿联酋、阿曼、也门等国接壤。海岸线长 2437 公里，领土面积位居世界第 14 位。

"沙特"取自于沙特阿拉伯王国的创始人伊本·沙特之名。而在阿拉伯语中，沙特是"幸福"的意思，"阿拉伯"则指"沙漠"，意为"幸福的沙漠"。伊斯兰教是沙特阿拉伯的国教，在沙特阿拉伯，全民信仰伊斯兰教。其中，逊尼派穆斯林占 85%，什叶派穆斯林占 15%。教徒一天必须祷告五次，祷告时当地人都必须要去清真寺做礼拜。女人必须穿黑袍。

沙特阿拉伯有四个首都。政治首都为利雅得。穆罕默德的诞生地麦加是沙特阿拉伯的宗教首都、文化首都，伊斯兰教的第一圣地，每年世界各地前往这里朝觐的穆斯林超过 300 万人。另外，沙特阿拉伯的夏都为塔伊夫；外交之都为吉达。

2014 年，沙特阿拉伯国内生产总值 7525 亿美元，增长率达 3.59%，人均国内生产总值 2.44 万美元。

1960 年，沙特阿拉伯加入 OPEC。石油工业是沙特阿拉伯经济的主要支柱。沙特阿拉伯以"石油王国"著称，是世界上石油储量、产量和销售量最多的国家之一。2005 年，沙特阿拉伯石油产量 5.26 亿吨，居世界第一位，出口石油 4.3 亿吨，剩余可采储量363亿吨（占全世界储量的26%），三项指标均居世界首位。2005年12月，沙特阿拉伯正式加入世界贸易组织。沙特阿拉伯受益于国际油价攀升，石油出口收入丰厚，占国家财政收入的70%以上，石化产品外销70多个国家和地区，石油出口占出口总额的93%。2014年，沙特阿拉伯石油产量为969万桶/日，全年石油2384亿美元。石油基础设施建设日趋完善，与其他国家之间也有便利的交通。比如，从达兰至黎巴嫩的赛达筑有中东最长的输油管（长1770公里），还有从东岸石油区到西岸的油管与液化气管道。

沙特阿拉伯的石油勘探工程中心是世界上最大最先进的科学研究设施之一，在中东地区更是首屈一指。广泛使用的三维地震探测技术，可以准确地划分新发现的油层的界线；运用横向钻探技术，使在困难地带和近海勘探成为可能。沙特阿拉伯最为成功的勘探是在中央阿拉伯地区。从这里开采出来的原油基本不含硫，并且很轻，用很低的成本就可以将原油精炼成具有高附加值的轻型产品。在尽力开发陆地原油生产潜力的同时，沙特阿拉伯还大力发展钻井平台技术，努力挖掘海上石油生产潜力。从20世纪60年代大规模勘探以来，沙特阿拉伯已经发现了约70个油气田，其中包括世界上最大的佳沃油田和世界上最大的海上油田——萨法尼亚油田。为了收集天然气，20世纪70年代沙特阿拉伯建造了万能天然气系统。该系统每日可收集加工1.3亿标准立方米的天然气，相当于为世界能源市场每日增加100多万桶的原油。红海沿岸的延布工业区和地处海湾的朱拜勒工业区的燃料、原料以及重要的公用设施的电力均来自于该系统。

现代化运输沙特阿拉伯石油管道输送系统在国内纵横交错，连通所有的加工厂和散货储存中心。东西走向的管道是横跨两个海岸的大动脉，将原油和液化气输送到全国各地以及国内各个工厂和两岸的装卸码头。沙特阿拉伯拥有世界上最新的原油运输船队，每艘船自重30多万吨，原油总运载量达200多万桶。

沙特阿拉伯政府利用石油收入，制定了庞大的经济发展计划，实行经济多样化政策，重点发展现代工业和基础工业，在充分利用本国丰富资源的同时积极引进国外先进技术和设备，以逐步改变单纯依赖石油收入的状况，建立现代化、多样化的国民经济体系，大力建设和改造国内基础和生产设施，继续推进经济结构多元化、劳动力本土化和经济私有化，大力发展钢铁、炼铝、水泥、海水淡化、电力工业、农业和服务业等非石油产业，鼓励发展农业、渔业和畜牧业，积极吸引外资，保护民族经济。

沙特阿拉伯天然气年产量640亿立方米，剩余可采储量6.9万亿立方米，占世界储量的4%，居世界第四位。沙特阿拉伯还有金、铜、铁、锡、铝、锌等矿藏。水资源以地下水为主。地下水总储量为36万亿立方米，按用水量计算，地表以下20米深的水源可使用320年左右。沙特阿拉伯是世界上最大的淡化海水生产国，其海水淡化量占世界总量的21%左右。沙特阿拉伯共有30个海水淡化厂，日产300万立方米淡化水，占全国饮用水的46%。沙特阿拉伯共有184个蓄水池，蓄水能力6.4亿立方米。沙特阿拉伯还出口有椰枣、畜产品；输入主要为粮食、糖、茶和纺织品等。

（二）伊拉克（Republic of Iraq）

伊拉克共和国位于亚洲西南部，阿拉伯半岛东北部，接壤的国家众多，在南方是沙特阿拉伯、科威特，北方是土耳其，西北是叙利亚，伊朗和约旦各位于其东西两侧。阿拉伯人约占全国总人口的73%，库尔德人约占21%。该国穆斯林约占人口的95%，其中什叶派穆斯林占54.5%、逊尼派穆斯林占40.5%。官方语言为阿拉伯语，北部库尔德地区的官方语言是库尔德语，东部地区有些居民讲波斯语。伊拉克所在的地区在历史上曾被称为美索不达米亚，是人类文明的主要发源地之一。首都，巴格达，同时也是伊拉克巴格达省的省会。巴格达人口约800万（2013年）。

伊拉克有悠久的历史，两河流域是世界古代文明的发祥地之一，公元前4700年就出现了城邦国家。公元前2000年先后建立被誉为“四大文明古国”之一的巴比伦王国、亚述帝国和新巴比伦王国。公元前500年为波斯帝国所灭。公元前4世纪被马其顿帝国侵占。公元7世纪时被阿拉伯帝国吞并并成为阿拉伯帝国的政治、文化中心。

2013年，伊拉克国内生产总值2250亿美元，人均国内生产总值6250美元，外汇储备725亿美元。2013年，伊拉克出口额901亿美元，进口额571亿美元。

1960年，伊拉克加入OPEC。伊拉克经济以石油业为主。伊拉克境内原油和天然气资源丰富，截至2013年，伊拉克探明石油储量202亿吨，居世界第5位。北部油区通过油管在黎巴嫩、叙利亚与土耳其的地中海港口输出原油，南部油田通过油管至沙特阿拉伯的红海岸延布油港输出原油。天然气储量约3.6万亿立方米，居世界第2位。磷酸盐储量约100亿吨。除了炼油与石油化工以外，伊拉克还发展纺织、食品、烟草、水泥等工业。

除了工业，农牧业在伊拉克也占重要地位。两河流域是伊拉克人口稠密，农业发达的地区，灌溉农业已有数千年历史，可耕地面积占国土总面积的27.6%，农业人口占全国总人口的三分之一。主要农产品有小麦、黑米、大麦、稻米、棉花、烟草、温带水果与椰枣等。椰枣输出量居世界首位。畜牧业偏重在东北部地区，养殖牛、羊、驴、马，西南部干旱高原上有游牧业。

（三）伊朗（Islamic Republic of Iran）

伊朗全名伊朗伊斯兰共和国，位于亚洲西部，属中东国家。伊朗中北部紧靠里海、南靠波斯湾和阿拉伯海。伊朗东邻巴基斯坦和阿富汗，东北部与土库曼斯坦接壤，西北与阿塞拜疆和亚美尼亚为邻，西界土耳其和伊拉克。国土面积约1648195平方公里，世界排名第十八。据伊朗国家统计数据库2014年7月18日显示，伊朗人口为77598379。伊朗是一个多民族的伊斯兰国家，其中波斯人占66%，阿塞拜疆人占25%，库尔德人占5%，还有阿拉伯人、巴赫蒂亚里人、卢尔人、俾路支人及土克曼人等少数民族。

伊朗是亚洲主要经济体之一。伊朗的经济实力位居亚洲第七位（次于中国、日本、印度、韩、印度尼西亚、沙特阿拉伯）。2013年，伊国内生产总值5148亿美元，人均国内生产总值6659美元。伊朗经济以石油开采业为主，石油化工、钢铁、汽车制造、电力、纺织、机械制造、食品加工、建材、地毯、家用电器、化工、冶金、造纸、水泥和制糖等也比较发达，但大部分原材料和零配件依赖进口。伊朗的电子工业、核工业、计算机软硬件业发展很快。

1960年，伊朗加入OPEC。伊朗盛产石油，是OPEC第二大石油输出国。截至2011年底，已探明石油储量1545.8亿桶，占世界总储量的11%，居世界第三，日产原油能力350

万桶。石油是伊朗经济命脉和外汇收入的主要来源之一，占伊朗外汇总收入的一半以上。胡齐斯坦为石油工业区与重要出海门户。

除了石油以外，其他资源也十分丰富。天然气蕴藏丰富，储量33.69万亿立方米，占世界总储量的17%，居世界第二位。天然气生产量列世界第四位，日产天然气5亿立方米。已探明矿山3800处，矿藏储量270亿吨；其中，铁矿储量47亿吨；铜矿储量30亿吨（矿石平均品位0.8%），约占世界总储量的5%，居世界第三位；锌矿储量2.3亿吨（平均品位20%），居世界第一位；铬矿储量2000万吨；金矿储量150吨。此外，还有大量的锰、锑、铅、硼、重晶石、大理石等矿产资源。目前，已开采矿种56个，年矿产量1.5亿吨，占总储量的0.55%，占全球矿产品总产量的1.2%。

农业在伊朗国民经济中占有重要地位。伊朗农耕资源丰富，全国可耕地面积超过5200万公顷，占其国土面积的30%以上，已耕面积1800万公顷，其中可灌溉耕地830万公顷，旱田940万公顷。农业人口占总人口的43%，农民人均耕地5.1公顷。农业机械化程度较低，其综合收割机与拖拉机保有量分别为1.3万台和36万台。近年来，伊政府高度重视、大力发展农业，目前粮食生产已实现90%自给自足。

伊朗主要出口商品为油气、金属矿石、皮革、地毯、水果、干果及鱼子酱等，主要进口产品有粮油食品、药品、运输工具、机械设备、牲畜、化工原料、饮料及烟草等。2012年，伊进出口总额约1787亿美元，其中出口额1117亿美元、同比下降21%，进口额670美元、同比下降7%。受制裁因素影响，2011年底以来，伊朗原油出口大幅下降。

近年来，旅游业在伊朗发展执着良好。伊朗拥有数千年文明史，自然地理和古代文明遗产丰富。从1991年起，政府开始致力发展旅游业，旅游业逐渐复苏，2013年3月至2014年3月，前往伊朗旅游及朝圣的外国人达400万，旅游收入50亿美元。伊朗全国有各类旅游组织、旅行社约3000个。德黑兰、伊斯法罕、设拉子、亚兹德、克尔曼、马什哈德是伊主要旅游地区。

（四）科威特（The State of Kuwait）

科威特全称科威特国，首都科威特城。科威特位于亚洲西部阿拉伯半岛东北部，波斯湾西北岸，西、北与伊拉克为邻，南部与沙特阿拉伯交界，东濒波斯湾科威特。面积17818平方公里（包括阿拉伯半岛的东北角及其附近的布比延、费莱凯等岛屿）。人口396.5万，其中科威特籍人124.3万（2014年），外国侨民主要有巴勒斯坦人、埃及人，其余为印度、伊朗、巴基斯坦和其他阿拉伯人。

2014年，科威特国内生产总值1810亿美元，人均国内生产总值7万美元，经济增长率2.3%，外贸总额1366亿美元（其中出口额1083亿美元，进口额283亿美元），外汇储备322亿美元。科威特石油和天然气储量丰富，石油和天然气工业是科威特国民经济主要支柱，石油和天然气产值占科威特国内生产总值的45%，占出口收入的92%。现已探明的石油储量140亿吨。南部的布尔干油田是世界上最大的砂岩油田，是仅次于加瓦尔油田的世界第二大油田。天然气储量为1.498万亿立方米，占世界储量的1.1%。天然气储量为1.78万亿立方米，居世界第18位。2014年原油日产量280万桶。科威特石油公司（Kuwait Petroleum Corporation）为世界十大石油公司之一，全面负责科国内外的原油和成品油销售。

1960 年，科威特加入 OPEC。科威特工业以石油开采、冶炼和石油化工为主，不仅在陆上开发，还开始开采丰富的海底气国。近年来，政府在重点发展石油、石化工业的同时，强调发展多元化经济，着力发展金融、贸易、旅游、会展等行业，并提出 2035 年发展愿景，将科威特建设成为地区商业和金融中心，发挥私营企业在科威特经济发展中的重要作用，保障人民生活全面均衡发展，实现社会公正。在 20 世纪第 2 个十年开始阶段，非石油生产产值占科威特国内生产总值的 60%，其中包括农、渔业 0.4%，制造业 13.3%，电气、水 0.1%，建筑业 2.7%，批发、零售 6.3%，餐饮旅馆业 0.8%，运输、仓储和通讯 4.6%，金融 4%，保险 0.2%，房地产和商务服务 7.3%，社区社会服务 22.4%等。

对外贸易在科威特在经济中占有重要地位。出口商品主要有石油、天然气和化工产品，进口商品有机械、运输设备、工业制品、粮食和食品等。主要贸易对象是：美国、日本、英国、韩国、意大利、德国、荷兰、新加坡等。国内有一座国际民用机场和两座军用机场。机场起降架次 3.3 万次/年，客流量 370 万人次/年，运货量 14 万吨/年。主要港口是舒威赫港和舒艾巴港。

（五）委内瑞拉（The Bolivarian Republic of Venezuela）

委内瑞拉玻利瓦尔共和国简称委内瑞拉。委内瑞拉的国名其实源自意大利文，是“小威尼斯”的意思，其典故出自意大利探险家阿美利哥·维斯普西（同时也是美洲的命名者）当初在马拉开波湖见到美洲印地安人所居住的水上高脚屋村落，联想到欧洲的水都威尼斯，因而如此命名。至于委内瑞拉正式全名里的“玻利瓦尔”，是 1999 年该国重修宪法时才加入，用以纪念被他们视为开国英雄的西蒙·玻利瓦尔。委内瑞拉人口2991万（2014年3月）。印欧混血种人占58%，白人29%，黑人11%，印第安人2%。官方语言为西班牙语，居民98%信奉天主教，1.5%信奉基督教。

委内瑞拉北临加勒比海与大西洋，东有圭亚那，南为巴西，西边则与哥伦比亚接壤，而在委内瑞拉外海则有阿鲁巴、荷属安地列斯（皆为荷兰的海外自治领土）与特立尼达和多巴哥等岛屿邦国。首都加拉加斯是个滨海的港口，也是该国最大城市。

委内瑞拉属拉丁美洲地区经济较为发达的国家之一。2013年，委内瑞拉国内生产总值4383亿美元，人均国内生产总值14523美元。

1960年，委内瑞拉加入OPEC。石油是委内瑞拉最主要矿物资源，储量约占世界储量的4%。截至2014年，委内瑞拉石油（含重油）探明储量为2984亿桶（约合409亿吨），居世界第一位。2014年，委石油日产量290万桶（约合41万吨），日出口量233万桶（约合33万吨）。因此，委内瑞拉不仅是南美第一产油国，而且是世界上重要的石油生产国和出口国。委内瑞拉境内主要的石油蕴藏区在其西北部的号称“拉丁美洲第一大湖”的马拉开波湖。在奥里诺科重质原油带探测到新石油资源，因此，奥里诺科成为委内瑞拉另一个重要的石油蕴藏区。石油工业在委内瑞拉经济中具有极其重要的地位，石油收入占全国财政总收入的70%以上。

除石油外，委内瑞拉其他矿产资源也很丰富。截至2014年，委内瑞拉天然气探明储量5.5万亿立方米，铁矿石探明储量36.44亿吨，煤炭探明储量7.28亿吨，铝矾土储量13.32亿吨，镍矿49万吨，黄金储量4353吨。此外，还有金刚石、铀、石灰岩等矿产资源。水力和森林资源也很丰富，森林覆盖率为56%。相应的，委内瑞拉主要工业部门有石油、铁矿、建筑、炼钢、炼铝、电力、汽车装配、食品加工、纺织等。其中石油部门为国民经济支柱产业，2013年石油业同比增长1.1%，非石油业同比增长2.1%。铁矿砂、铝矾土和黄金也是委内瑞拉主要工业产品。

1990年9月，委内瑞拉加入“关税和贸易总协定”，现与世界100多个国家和地区有贸易关系。主要出口原油、石油化工产品、铝锭、钢材、铁矿砂、金属制品等，进口机电设备、化工和五金产品、汽车配件、建筑材料及农产品等。主要贸易对象为美国、中国、哥伦比亚、巴西和墨西哥。2013年，委内瑞拉外贸总额1105亿美元（其中，进口总额437亿美元，出口总额669亿美元），外汇储备205亿美元。

委内瑞拉是受全世界游客欢迎的国家。著名游览点为安赫尔瀑布和玛格丽塔岛等。2013年，委内瑞拉共接待外国游客64.38万人次，游客主要来自哥伦比亚，巴西，美国等国。

（六）卡塔尔（The State of Qatar）

卡塔尔国简称卡塔尔，是亚洲西部的一个阿拉伯国家，位于波斯湾西南岸的卡塔尔半岛上，与阿联酋和沙特阿拉伯接壤。海岸线长550公里。首都多哈，也叫贝达，是全国第一大城市和政治、经济、交通和文化中心，是波斯湾著名港口之一。卡塔尔国土面积11521平方公里。人口212万（2013年），其中多数在油田工作。本国居民为阿拉伯人，外籍人口数约占人口总数的84%，主要来自印度、巴基斯坦和东南亚国家。阿拉伯语为官方语言。卡塔尔属热带沙漠气候，夏天最高气温可达46℃；冬季凉爽干燥，最低气温7℃。年平均降水量仅125毫米。

1994年，卡塔尔成为关贸总协定第121个成员，1995年成为世界贸易组织成员。2014年，卡塔尔国内生产总值1980亿美元，经济增长率6%，人均国内生产总值9.3万美元，进出口总额1563亿美元（其中进口额382亿美元，出口额1181亿美元）。

1961年，卡塔尔加入OPEC。卡塔尔已探明石油储量25亿吨，居世界第13位。相比较贫乏的地下水，在卡塔尔油比水贵。石油部门在卡塔尔工业中地位重要，相关产业如炼油厂、石化工厂等比较发达。石油的主要销售航线有3条，分别是马六甲路线、苏伊士航线、地中海航线，其中最便捷的则是苏伊士航线。

卡塔尔的天然气储量24.7万亿立方米，居世界第3位，年产能达7900万吨。卡塔尔不仅是中东重要的液化天然气出口国，甚至是世界第一大液化天然气生产和出口国。卡塔尔政府大力投资开发天然气，将其作为经济发展的重中之重。

此外，卡塔尔还将展非石油、天然气工业，作为实现国民收入多元化和摆脱对石油依赖的主要途径，建了造纸厂、洗涤剂厂、颜料厂、食品厂和塑料厂等。注重吸引外资和技术；鼓励发展农业，免费向农民提供种子、化肥和农业机械，号召植树造林，扩大耕地面积。

卡塔尔有5个机场，多哈国际机场有连接欧洲和亚洲的20余条航线。2005年对外贸易总额为301亿美元，其中进口67亿美元，出口234亿美元。主要出口石油、液化气、合成氨、尿素、乙烯等。进口产品主要是机械和运输设备、食品、工业原材料及轻工产品、药品等。主要贸易伙伴有美国、日本及西欧国家。

（七）利比亚（State of Libya）

利比亚国简称利比亚，是北非的一个国家，位于地中海南岸，与埃及、苏丹、乍得、尼日尔、阿尔及利亚、突尼斯相邻。面积 175.95 万平方公里。海岸线长约 1900 余公里。全境 95％以上地区为沙漠和半沙漠。主要港口有的黎波里、班加西、图布鲁克、卜雷加、德尔纳、米苏拉塔、扎维亚、拉斯拉努夫。人口 715 万（2014 年预测），主要是阿拉伯人，其他为柏柏尔人。绝大多数居民信仰伊斯兰教，逊尼派穆斯林占 97.2％。阿拉伯语为国语，在主要城市也讲英语、意大利语。严格遵循伊斯兰教传统的利比亚大多数的妇女都习惯披戴头巾再出门。

2014 年，利比亚国内生产总值 642 亿美元，人均国内生产总值 10094 美元。

1962 年，利比亚加入 OPEC。利比亚是主要的石油出口国之一，石油探明储量为 430 亿桶。20 世纪 50 年代发现石油后，1955 年利比亚颁布《国家石油法》，并开始石油勘探，石油开采及炼油工业发展迅速。1959 年发现了第一批油田，1961 年开始出口原油。2004 年，利比亚原油产量达到 160 万桶/日，国内消费约 25 万桶/日，净出口约 120 万桶/日（2012）（2004 年 6 月恢复对美出口石油），出口占总产量的 83.75％。利比亚原油油质好，并且含硫量低，蜡油产率高。利比亚油田通过管道网络接至地中海。利比亚国家石油公司拥有 7 条输油管道，有 6 个石油储备基地，并还在筹划扩建石油储备和炼油基地。石油是利的经济命脉和主要支柱，石油生产占国民生产总值的 50％—70％，石油出口占出口总值的 95％以上。2012 年出口石油创汇达 516 亿美元，主要出口至意大利、德国、西班牙、法国等国。

除石油外，利比亚的天然气储量也较多，探明储量达1.54万亿立方米。其他资源有铁（蕴藏量20亿—30亿吨）、钾、锰、磷酸盐、铜、锡、硫磺、铝矾土等，但这些资源开发较少。沿海水产主要有金枪鱼、沙丁鱼、海绵等。

利比亚主要工业部门是石油开采、炼油，还有食品加工、石化、化工、建材、发电、采矿、纺织业等。

2014年，利比亚出口额为289亿美元，进口额为153亿美元。利比亚主要出口产品是石油、铁矿石、花生、皮革等，产量80%以上供出口。主要进口粮食、食品、机械、建材、运输设备、电器、化工和轻工产品以及武器装备。主要贸易对象是意大利、中国、土耳其等。

（八）阿拉伯联合酋长国（The United Arab Emirates）

阿拉伯联合酋长国简称阿联酋，位于阿拉伯半岛东部，北濒波斯湾，西北与卡塔尔为邻，西和南与沙特阿拉伯交界，东和东北与阿曼毗连海岸线长734公里，首都阿布扎比，也是境内最大部族的领地。本地居民为阿拉伯人，外籍人口约占3/4，主要来自印度、巴基斯坦等国。居民大多信奉伊斯兰教，多数属逊尼派；在迪拜，什叶派占多数。

阿联酋是一个沙漠国家，有“沙漠中的花朵”的美称。阿联酋包括七个酋长国：阿布扎比、迪拜、沙迦、阿治曼、乌姆盖万、拉斯海马酋长国、富吉拉，各部落有各自的自主行政权，包括邮政服务。

2014年，阿联酋国内生产总值4197亿美元，增长率4.6%，人均GDP 7.2万美元，进出口总额6339亿美元（其中进口额2536亿美元，出口额3803亿美元），外汇储备759

亿美元。

1967 年，阿联酋加入 OPEC。阿联酋以石油生产和石油化工工业为主。阿联酋的石油和天然气资源非常丰富。1958 年阿联酋石油生产起步，1962 年开始出口石油，迄今已成为世界重要原油生产国和出口国。已探明石油储量 130 亿吨，天然气储量 6.1 万亿立方米。2012 年原油日产量 269 万桶，计划于 2018 年提高到 350 万桶。阿联酋的石油业自 20 世纪 60 年代由荷兰皇家壳牌集团、英国石油公司、道达尔公司等世界级大石油公司发展建设起来后，阿联酋逐渐通过控股实现石油国有化。1988 年，阿成立最高石油委员会，负责制定油气相关政策，颁布有关油气生产的决议，由外国参股公司负责技术、生产和管理。最高石油委员会同本国和国际上有实力的能源公司建立了新型战略伙伴或战略同盟关系。与该委员会合作密切的公司有：荷兰皇家壳牌集团、道达尔公司、英国石油公司、埃克森美孚公司、葡萄牙石油天然气公司、日本石油株式会社等。阿联酋生产的原油大部分用于出口。

阿联酋政府在发展石化工业的同时，把发展多样化经济、扩大贸易和增加非石油收入在国内生产总值中的比重作为首要任务，努力发展水泥、炼铝、塑料制品、建筑材料、服装、食品加工等工业，重视发展农、牧、渔业；充分利用各种财源，重点发展文教、卫生事业。近年来，大力发展以信息技术为核心的知识经济，同时注重可再生能源研发，首都阿布扎比于 2009 年 6 月获选国际可再生能源署总部所在地。

1995 年，阿联酋加入世界贸易组织。外贸在经济中占有重要位置。阿联酋主要出口石油、天然气、石油化工产品、铝锭和少量土特产品；主要进口粮食、机械和消费品。

（九）阿尔及利亚（People's Democratic Republic of Algeria）

阿尔及利亚民主人民共和国，简称阿尔及利亚，位于非洲西北部。北临地中海，东临突尼斯、利比亚，南与尼日尔、马里和毛里塔尼亚接壤，西与摩洛哥、西撒哈拉交界。南北线长约 2000 千米，东西最宽约 1800 千米，海岸线长约 1200 公里。人口 3790 万（2013 年）。大多数是阿拉伯人，其次是柏柏尔人（约占总人口 20%）。少数民族有姆扎布族和图阿雷格族。官方语言为阿拉伯语，通用语言为法语。

2014 年，阿尔及利亚国内生产总值 2109 亿美元，经济增长率 3%，人均国内生产总值 5394 美元，外贸总额 1199 亿美元（其中进口额 582 亿美元，出口额 617 亿美元），外汇储备 1829 亿美元。阿尔及利亚经济规模在非洲居第四位，仅次于南非、尼日利亚和埃及。

21 世纪初阿尔及利亚执行了 2005 年至 2009 年“五年经济社会振兴规划”及南部、高原省份经济发展计划，政府斥资近 1440 亿美元用于国企改造和基础设施建设。2005 年以来，国际油价走高，阿尔及利亚油气收入大增，经济稳步增长，经济重建全面开展。政府一方面继续实施财政扩张政策，加快大型基础设施建设，推动国有企业和金融体系改革，加大对中小企业的扶持；一方面扩大经济开放，出台“新碳化氢法”鼓励外企参与阿油气开发，密切与欧、美的经贸合作，加紧开展“入世”谈判。

1969 年，阿尔及利亚加入 OPEC。石油与天然气行业是阿尔及利亚国民经济的支柱，油气产业占国内生产总值 45.1%。石油探明储量约 17 亿吨，占世界总储量 1%，居世界第15位，主要是撒哈拉轻质油，油质较高。天然气探明可采储量4.58万亿立方米，占世界总储量的2.37%，居世界第10位。石油和天然气工业是首要经济部门，石油开采量居非洲前列，石油和天然气占出口总值95%以上。阿尔及利亚油气产品大部分出口。

阿尔及利亚其他矿藏主要有铁、铅锌、铀、铜、金、磷酸盐、磷灰石等。其中铁矿储量为30亿—50亿吨，主要分布在东部乌昂扎矿和布哈德拉矿。铅锌矿储量估计为1.5亿吨，铀矿5万吨，磷酸盐20亿吨，黄金100吨。阿尔及利亚水利资源丰富，可开发水资源约172亿立方米，水坝64座，蓄水能力710亿立方米。

阿尔及利亚其他工业有食品、纺织、化工、钢铁、农机等。多半人口从事农业。主要经济作物是葡萄、柑橘、蔬菜，粮食作物有小麦、大麦等。牲畜多绵羊、山羊。盛产栓皮栎和阿尔法草。葡萄酒、柑橘、蔬菜、橄榄油、软木、阿尔法草均是传统出口商品。进口以机械设备、工业品、日用品和食品为大宗。主要部门有能矿、钢铁、冶金、机械、电力等。主要贸易伙伴是西方工业国。政府鼓励非碳化氢产品出口，主张贸易多元化。

阿尔及利亚旅游资源丰富，全境有7处自然、文化景点被联合国教科文组织列为世界遗产。

（十）尼日利亚（Federal Republic of Nigeria）

尼日利亚联邦共和国，简称尼日利亚，处于西非东南部的国家，非洲几内亚湾西岸的顶点，邻国包括西边的贝宁，北边的尼日尔，东北方隔乍得湖与乍得接壤一小段国界，东和东南与喀麦隆毗连，南濒大西洋几内亚湾。尼日利亚海岸线长800

公里。地势北高南低。国土面积923，768平方公里。人口1.8亿（2014年）。非洲人口最多的国家。有250多个民族，其中最大的是北部的豪萨－富拉尼族（占全国人口29%）、西部的约鲁巴族（占21%）和东部的伊博族（占18%）。官方语言为英语。主要民族语言有豪萨语、约鲁巴语和伊博语。居民中50%信奉伊斯兰教，40%信奉基督教，10%信仰其他宗教。

1992年，尼日利亚被国际货币基金组织列为低收入国家。1995年起，政府对经济进行整顿并取得了一定成效。1998年，由于国际市场油价下跌和国内炼油厂停产，经济增速减慢。1999年奥巴桑乔上台后，积极推行自由化和私有化改革，实施紧缩的货币政策，严格限制举借新债，大力扶持农业，加强石油、天然气、矿业等产业的发展和基础设施建设，积极争取外资、外援和债务减免。由于国际市场油价持续上扬这一有利的外部因素，尼日利亚经济形势趋于好转。尼日利亚原来是农业国，但在20世纪下开始农业日渐萎缩。20世纪70年代起，石油出口逐渐成为主要经济来源。随着石油经济的发展，尼日利亚成为非洲最大的石油生产国、世界第六大石油出口国、非洲第一大经济体，2013年经济总量全球排名第26位。2014年，尼日利亚国内生产总值5799亿美元，经济增长率6.3%，人均国内生产总值3452美元。

1971年，尼日利亚加入OPEC。石油工业是尼日利亚国民经济的支柱。已探明石油储量372亿桶，居世界第10、非洲第2位。已探明天然气储量达5.3万亿立方米，居非洲第一。尼日利亚联邦政府财政收入的85%、国内生产总值的20%—30%来源于石油行业，石油出口收入总出口总收入的98%。2013年，尼日利亚日产原油194万桶，居非洲第一，原油出口收入约为840亿美元。2014年日产原油约为225万桶/天，上半年原油出口收入约为400亿美元。因国内炼油能力较低，约85%国内成品油消费需依赖进口。

为改变经济对石油工业的过多依赖，尼日利亚政府已实施天然气开发战略，大力开发国内丰富的天然气资源，以达到推动经济发展和增加政府收入的目的。煤储量约27.5亿吨，为西非唯一产煤国。尼日利亚的宝石开采兴盛了多年，主要包括蓝宝石、红宝石、海蓝宝石、祖母绿、电气石、黄宝石、石榴石和锆石等品种。

尼日利亚主要制造业为纺织、车辆装配、木材加工、水泥、饮料和食品加工。基础设施年久失修，技术水平较低，多数工业制品仍依赖进口。农业在国内生产总值中占40%。全国70%的劳动力从事农业。农业主要产区集中在北方地区。农业生产方式仍以小农经济为主，粮食不能自给，每年仍需大量进口。

尼日利亚资源丰富。已探明有30多种矿藏。主要有石油、天然气、锡、煤、石灰石、矾土、钽铁矿、黄金、铁矿石、锡、铌、石墨和锌等。煤储量约27.5亿吨，为西非唯一产煤国。尼日利亚有很多还未被大规模开发的矿物资源，包括天然气、煤、石灰石。尽管这些自然资源有很大的储量，但尼日利亚的采掘工业还处于初级阶段。

尼日利亚旅游资源丰富，如瀑布、海滩、赤道森林等。多数旅游点管理不善，游客很少。主要旅游景点有奥逊州的奥索博神树林，阿达玛瓦州的宿库卢文化遗产，夸拉州的奥乌瀑布，博尔诺州的乍得湖寺院，十字河流州的奥布都大牧场，伊莫州的奥古都湖，翁多州的温泉和包奇州的杨卡里野生动物园。

（十一）厄瓜多尔（The Republic of Ecuador）

厄瓜多尔全称厄瓜多尔共和国，位于南美洲的西北部，北与哥伦比亚相邻，南接秘鲁，西滨太平洋，与智利同为南美洲不与巴西相邻的国家，另辖有距厄瓜多尔本土 1000 公里的加拉帕戈斯群岛，原为印加帝国一部分。西班牙语意为“赤道”。别称有“赤道之国”、“香蕉之国”。人口 1596 万（2013 年）。其中，印欧混血种人占 77.42%，印第安人占 6.83%，白种人占 10.46%，黑白混血种人占 2.74%，黑人和其他人种占 2.55%。官方语言为西班牙语，印第安人通用克丘亚语。94%的居民信奉天主教。首都基多位于皮钦查火山的山麓，高达 2850 米的海拔，使该市成为全世界第二高的首都，仅次于玻利维亚首都拉巴斯。

2013 年，厄瓜多尔国内生产总值 669 亿美元，经济增长率 3.4%，人均国内生产总值 5627 美元，外汇储备 32 亿美元。

厄瓜多尔工业主要有石油和采矿业、制造业、建筑和电力工业等。2011 年，制造业、建筑业、采矿业产值分别为 57.78 亿美元、72.26 亿美元和 89.95 亿美元。

厄瓜多尔加入 OPEC 的过程最复杂。1973 年第一次加入，1992 年退出，2007 年再次加入。厄瓜多尔矿物以石油为主，主要分布于瓜亚基尔湾一带，在亚马孙平原地区也发现有油田。石油是厄瓜多尔重要的经济支柱。石油探明储量为 82.4 亿桶。2014 年，厄瓜多尔石油产量为 2.03 亿桶。

除石油外，厄瓜多尔其他自然资源也较丰富。天然气储量 2250 亿立方米。此外还有金、银、铜、铁、锰、煤、硫黄等。森林覆盖率 42.5%。水力和渔业资源也丰富。

旅游业是厄瓜多尔的第四大创汇行业，约有50万人直接或间接从事旅游业。2014年，厄瓜多尔接待外国旅游者150万人次。外国游客主要来自美国、哥伦比亚、秘鲁和西班牙。主要旅游点有基多、瓜亚基尔、昆卡、因巴布拉省、东部亚马孙河流域和加拉帕戈斯群岛（龟岛）。基多市、龟岛和昆卡市被联合国教科文组织列入“世界文化与自然遗产”名录。

（十二）安哥拉（The Republic of Angola）

安哥拉共和国简称安哥拉，位于非洲西南部，首都罗安达。安哥拉西滨大西洋，北及东北邻刚果民主共和国，南邻纳米比亚，东南邻赞比亚，另有一块外飞地卡宾达省与刚果共和国、刚果民主共和国相邻。人口2100万（2014年估值）。主要有奥温本杜（约占总人口的38%）、姆本杜（25%）、巴刚果（14%）、隆达等民族。全国平均人口密度为16人/平方公里，首都罗安达人口密度最大，卡宾达人口密度最小。官方语言为葡萄牙语，有42种民族语言，主要民族语言有温本杜语（中部和南部地区）、金本杜语（罗安达和内陆地区）和基孔戈语（北部地区）等。49%的人信奉罗马天主教，13%的人信奉基督教新教，其余人口大多信奉原始宗教。

安哥拉曾经属于最不发达国家。2002年后，安哥拉政府将工作重点转向经济恢复和社会发展，调整经济结构，大力投入基础设施建设，优先解决关系国计民生的社会发展项目；同时积极开展同其他国家的经贸互利合作，努力为国家重建吸引外资。安哥拉现已成为撒哈拉以南非洲第三大经济体和最大引资国之一。2014年，安哥拉国内生产总值1330.5亿美元，增长率：4.1%，人均国内生产总值（按购买力平价计算）8118美元，外汇储备279亿美元。

2007年，安哥拉加入OPEC。安哥拉的石油、天然气和矿产资源丰富。安哥拉已探明石油可采储量超过137亿桶，天然气储量达7万亿立方米。石油和钻石开采是国民经济的支柱产业，安哥拉是非洲第二大产油国。2007年，安哥拉加入石油输出国组织。随着国际市场原油价格的攀升，安石油出口收入大幅增加。据国际货币基金组织统计，2001—2010年安经济年均增长率为11.1%，居全球第一。2013年原油产量6.261亿桶，平均日产173万桶，石油业产值占安国内生产总值的40%。

安哥拉主要矿产有钻石、铁、磷酸盐、铜、锰、铀、铅、锡、锌、钨、黄金、石英、大理石和花岗岩等。安哥拉钻石储量约10亿克拉，2011年原钻产量833万克拉，为世界第五大钻石生产国。安哥拉铁矿17亿吨，磷酸盐2亿吨，锰矿近1亿吨。森林面积5300万公顷，森林覆盖率43%，是非洲第二大林业资源国，出产乌木、非洲白檀木、紫檀木、桃花心木等名贵木材。安哥拉主要工业还有水泥、建材、车辆组装和修理、纺织服装、食品和水产加工等。

安哥拉土地肥沃，河流密布，发展农业的自然条件良好。农牧渔业发展非常好。

2010年，安哥拉接待游客42.5万人，游客主要来自欧洲（40%），美洲（19.5%）和非洲（18.1%），旅游业收入约10亿美元。安哥拉建立了国家公园和保护区，如罗安达省奎卡玛国家公园、莱多角旅游区，马兰热省卡兰杜拉旅游区，宽多库帮戈省奥卡万戈旅游区，莫西科省卡米亚国家公园等。安哥拉与赞比亚、津巴布韦、博茨瓦纳和纳米比亚建立了跨境自然环境保护区。大黑羚羊（Black Antelopes）是安哥拉独有的动物，也是安哥拉国家的标志和象征。